# Credit Card Usury and The Christian Failure to Stop It

*A Call to Social Justice against the Money Changers*

**Second Edition**

Copyright © November 2010 by Paul Peter Jesep
All Rights Reserved – Second Edition

In Memory of

Hryhorij Savyc Skovoroda
(1722-1794)

*I thank God that he made everything necessary easy and only the unnecessary difficult.*

# Contents

| | |
|---|---:|
| Acknowledgments | 5 |
| Call to Action | 7 |
| Sacralization and Commoditization | 21 |
| Social Impact | 29 |
| - Consequences | 29 |
| - Personal and Corporate Responsibility | 55 |
| Eucharist | 58 |
| - Justice | 61 |
| - My Sister and Brother's Keeper | 67 |
| - Forgiveness | 68 |
| - Thirst for Righteousness | 73 |
| - The Lord's Prayer | 80 |
| - Full Circle | 84 |
| Living the Faith | 86 |
| Bibliography | 93 |
| Index | 120 |
| Scriptural References | 124 |
| Links and Resources | 125 |
| About the Author | 128 |

# Acknowledgments

Professors Glenn Miller and Marvin Ellison of Bangor Theological Seminary (BTS) provided invaluable and necessary feedback to this project that started out as my graduate thesis. It is a better work due to their involvement. Their time, insights, knowledge, and no doubt the patience needed to review drafts of the thesis were never taken for granted. It should especially be noted that since their sign-off on what was the thesis, information has been added with more analysis. Any errors or limitations that may exist are mine.

Fr. William Jerome Myers of Louisville, Kentucky, was always there and provided some of the emotional support to get me through the experience. I kvetched. He listened. I sulked. He remained positive. I procrastinated. He kept me focused. I growled. He teased. I snorted. He laughed. I was befuddled. He cleared things up. I finally finished. He kveled. I ate pastry. Thanks, Will.

Conversations with Dick Rozek of Portsmouth, New Hampshire over several years fueled this topic. He always provided good insights on the subject when I was a columnist living in the Granite State and afterwards. Dick is honorable, thoughtful, intellectual, and extraordinarily insightful. He has been a steadfast friend and supporter. Thanks, Dick.

This endeavor also reflects my experiences at a wonderful, extraordinary institution, Bangor Theological Seminary (BTS.edu). I had the opportunity to study at its Portland, Maine and Bangor campuses. BTS will always have a special place in my heart.

I am especially grateful to The Rev. Dr. Glenn Miller who made my time at BTS particularly special and memorable. The insights and personal experiences he shared with me on art, dance, faith, music, and religion were extraordinarily enriching. Thanks, Comrade.

Lastly, Laurie McQuarrie, BTS Librarian, played an important and necessary role in bringing the thesis to its completion. She went above and beyond the call of duty in formatting it. Her formatted version of the thesis served as the foundation for the book.

# Call to Action

Over 2,000 years ago Jesus shared values, teachings, and a way of life when there were no credit cards and collection agencies. Nor were there arbitrary credit or Fair, Isaac and Company (FICO) scores which are now used to determine eligibility for employment, car loans, home ownership, student loans, and apartment rentals. The interconnected industries of banks, credit bureaus, and collection agencies have an enormous impact on the spiritual, emotional, and physical well-being of families and individuals.

Darwinian capitalism, evidenced in part by an absence of corporate ethics and responsibility, has caused a human rights crisis and many religious leaders do nothing about it. Fortunately, some are beginning to see the magnitude that debt has on the spiritual, emotional, and physical lives of their parishioners.[1] Individual and collective consumer debt, which provides banks with a permanent, if not long-term revenue source, is increasingly being compared to modern slavery[2] or

---

[1] But see Rev. Timothy Fountain, "My Voice: Loss of Credit Card Jobs Sign of Better Times," ArgusLeader.com, September 17, 2010. Rev. Fountain offers a personal perspective about credit card exploitation in a state where the industry has done quite well.

[2] Matthew Scott, "Is Debt a New Form of Slavery?" DailyFinance.com, October 21, 2010.

debt-serfdom.[3] As banks exploit or enslave consumers executives in the financial services industries are expected to receive a record $144 billion in benefits and compensation in 2010. It is a 4% increase over last year.[4]

In light of the harm these industries are causing to families and individuals that range from arrests to driving some to suicide a response is needed comparable to Jesus chasing the money changers out of the temple (Mark 11:15-19, 11:27-33; Matthew 21:12-17, 21:23-2; Luke 19:45-48, 20:1-8; John 2:13-16).

Greater discussion is required by Christian and non–Christian social justice advocates regarding government oversight and ongoing industry practices that impact equity and unjust gain. Although economies and political systems have evolved from the time of Jesus; lending, borrowing, and the allowable rate of interest have been integral for much of modern history.[5]

---

[3] Charles Hugh Smith, "Dear 'Middle Class' Americans: Most of you are Debt Serfs with Zero Assets," BusinessInsider.com, October 12, 2010.

[4] See Liz Rappaport, Aaron Lucchetti and Stephen Grocer, "Wall Street Pay: A Record $144 Billion," WSJ.com, October 11, 2010. The $144 billion figure includes banks, hedge funds, securities exchanges, investment banks, and money-management organizations.

[5] According to J. Duncan M. Derrett, the lender during the time of Jesus had "discretion to show grace and favor." Terms were dependent upon the nature of the relationship. Derrett identified three types of loans: for use; for consumption; and for business with lending to non-Jews at interest. Bruce M. Metzger and Michael D. Coogan, eds., *The Oxford Companion to the Bible* (Oxford: Oxford University Press, 1993), 463

Christian[6] ethical models are needed to evaluate the policies and repercussions of loaning and the charging of interest.[7] The meaning of corporate responsibility and good corporate citizenship must be discussed. Although the focus here is on the conduct of collection agencies, credit bureaus, and credit card companies, Christian ethicists should include at some point mortgages, car loans, and student loan debt. Education debt now exceeds $829 billion which, for the first time in

---

[6] In light of the silence toward and participation in many injustices by "Christians" the word "Christian" is increasingly irrelevant. Although it goes beyond the focus of this book, it is worth raising that Christianity has become so corporate, so "un-Christian" that perhaps it would be better to refer to social justice advocates in the spirit of Christ as "followers of Jesus."

[7] Aristotle called usury "the breeding of money." He added that "usury is money bred of money . . . of all forms of money-making it is most against nature." *Politics* (Charleston: BiblioBazaar, 1928), 48. In the Hebrew Scriptures "usury" is the charging of any interest. See Richard Johnston's essay, *Usury: Why Should I Show Interest?* in *Voices from the University: The Legacy of the Hebrew Bible*, Heidi M. Szpek, ed. (Bloomington: iUniverse, 2002), 275. See also Rabbi Meir Orlian, "The Usury Suspects," (printed September 22, 2010), CommunityM.com. Martin Luther observed that "Greed and usury have burst in like a great flood and have attained a semblance of legality." *Martin Luther's Basic Theological Writings* (Minneapolis: Augsburg Fortress, 2005), 339. In the Nineteenth Century Henry Campbell Black defined usury as "an illegal rate of interest . . . A usurious loan is one whose interest rates are determined to be in excess of those permitted by the usury laws." It can, however, also be an "unconscionable and exorbitant rate or amount of interest." Thus it's legal, but unconscionable. *Black's Law Dictionary – 6th Edition* (St. Paul: West Publishing, 1990).

In Dante's *Inferno* usurers were placed below murderers in the seventh circle.

history, is higher than revolving credit which stands at $826.5 billion owed[8]

According to a money advice coordinator in the United Kingdom, if credit card rates were capped and reduced short-term consumer debt could drop by as much as fifty percent.[9] In July 2010, Elizabeth Warren, Harvard professor and originator of the Consumer Financial Protection Bureau said that "Meaningful rules in the consumer credit market can accelerate

---

[8] "Student-Loan Debt Surpasses Credit Cards," *Wall Street Journal*, (blogs.wsj.com), August 9, 2010. Student loan debt is another injustice that Christian leaders should address. Students are encouraged to "invest in their future" by taking out massive amounts of loans despite the hard reality that they will not earn a suitable income to pay off the debt with any ease. Like those with credit cards, graduates will become a cash cow, a long-term revenue source for banks. See in general "Young People Struggle to Deal with Kiss of Debt," USAToday.com, November 22, 2006; "TransUnion: Student Loan Delinquencies Down this Quarter, but Rise Year Over Year," MarketWatch.com, April 27, 2010; Christine Dugas, "Generation Y's Steep Financial Hurdles: Huge Debt, No Savings," USAToday.com, April 23, 2010; David Randall, "More Graduates Defaulting on their Student Loans," http://blogs.forbes.com/moneybuilder/2010/05/04/more-graduates-defaulting-on-their-student-loans/, May 4, 2010; Peter S. Goodman, "In Hard Times, Lured Into Trade School and Debt," NYTimes.com, March 13, 2010; and Jonathan D. Glater, "Finding Debt a Bigger Hurdle Than Bar Exam," NYTimes.com, July 2, 2009.

For an eye-opening account of the student loan crisis see Stephanie Kraft, "Killer Loans-Student Loan Borrowers Drown in Debt as Lenders Make Billions," http://valleyadvocate.com/article_print.cfm?aid=12585, October 14, 2010. See also StudentLoanJustice.org, ForgiveStudentLoadDebt.com, BankruptYourStudentLoans.com, and ProjectOnStudentDebt.org.

See also Adam Rodewald, "Student Loan Debt Now Exceeds Credit Cards," TheNorthWestern.com, October 21, 2010.

[9] "Credit Card Debt 'Could be Halved by Interest Rate Cap'," WHICH4U.co.uk, October 20, 2010.

economic recovery" in the United States.[10] It appears that consumer debt is a factor in the decline of America's middle class.[11] It contributes to economic inequality.[12]

Warren further told interviewer Lynn Parramore that by better keeping banks in check consumers will be less exploited and have more money in their pockets. This economic freedom along with other legal oversight will free and empower average Americans to weed "out all the tricks and traps that sap families of billions of dollars annually."[13]

In September 2010, President Obama appointed Prof. Warren as a special assistant to oversee the Bureau's creation. He chose not to appoint her its new director fearing bank lobbyists would successfully exert enough pressure in the U.S. Senate to block her confirmation.[14]

One of Warren's top priorities is to make credit card agreements understandable. According to CreditCards.com, 4 out of 5 Americans cannot read the average consumer

---

[10] Lynn Parramore, "Exclusive Interview: Elizabeth Warren Says Big Banks Must Stop Blocking Reform," Huffingtonpost.com, July 12, 2010.

[11] Bruce Watson, "Disturbing Statistics on the Decline of America's Middle Class," DailyFinance.com, October 17, 2010.

[12] See in general, Robert H. Frank, "Income Inequality: Too Big to Ignore," NYTimes.com, October 16, 2010.

[13] Parramore, "Exclusive Interview: Elizabeth Warren Says Big Banks Must Stop Blocking Reform."

[14] David Jackson, "Obama Looks to Avoid Fight Over New Consumer Agency," USAToday.com, September 16, 2010.

agreement. A grammar expert pointed out that "dense prose is used to confuse."[15]

Although not yet widely identified or understood as a human rights issue, the predatory consumer credit game that Prof. Warren has written about and spoken out against for many years can and does impact the ability to live with dignity. Christians have been remarkably silent, complacent, or oblivious to consumer credit exploitation as a human rights issue. Is there no Christian responsibility to take action?

Today, state and federal laws in the United States permit credit card interest rates to exceed 79%.[16] First Premier Bank Mastercard set 79% rate last year. This year, however, it offers an APR of 23.9% to 59.9%. This does not include fees. First Premier will also increase a consumer's credit limit at $50 for every $100 increase.[17] During the last week of July 2009, Citibank sent notices to credit card holders informing them that interest rates would increase to 29.99%.[18]

---

[15] Herb Weisbaum, "Warren's Top Goal: Keeping Credit Simple," September 22, 2010, MSNBC.com.

[16] "First PREMIER Bankcard Offers Customer 79.9% APR Credit Card," October 15, 2009, AmericanBankingNews.com.

[17] "Worst: First Premier Bank Mastercard," ConsumerReports.org, November 2010.

[18] Jennifer Dewait, "No Brainer," CreditTrak.com, July 31, 2009. Most credit cards have rates between 12-21%. See William Davis, "Average Credit Card Rates Higher than 14 Percent," CreditNet.com, October 12, 2010.

In July 2009, the average credit card debt for low and middle class families reached $9,800. One out of three families uses credit cards to cover basic living expenses.[19]

Henry Campbell Black defined usury as exceeding an interest rate permitted by law. He also defined it as something that could be legal yet "unconscionable and exorbitant."[20] Prof. Warren identifies that the plight of the middle class has been fueled by the credit industry that has "drained billions of dollars out of their pockets."[21]

Does this reflect an economy that "works for people" or one that requires them to work for it?[22] In working for the economy who is the beneficiary? How does a family or individual get out of ever increasing debt caused by this financial structure?

Not only has it created a new form of bondage and long-term, if not permanent, revenue source for banks, but forgotten in a self-described Judeo-Christian nation is that "you were a slave in the land of Egypt, and the Lord your God

---

[19] Julia Spencer, "Financial Edge," CreditTrak.com, July 29, 2009.

[20] Black's Law Dictionary (St. Paul: West Publishing Co., 1990), 1545.

[21] David S. Morgan, "Warren: Middle Class Has Suffered for 30 Years," September 21, 2010, CBSNews.com.

[22] See Chuck Collins and Mary Wright, *The Moral Measure of the Economy* (Maryknoll: Orbis Books, 2007), 6 & 59.

redeemed you; for this reason I lay this command upon you today" to show mercy (Deuteronomy 15:15; Leviticus 25:42-43).

What are the consequences for such commercial relationships? Is a 29.99% rate on a balance not paid off each month greed or unjust gain? Is this a zealous pursuit of excessive gain (Proverbs 23:4; 28:20)? Does it suggest oppression (Jeremiah 15:10)? In 2009, a defeated piece of legislation in the U.S. Senate suggested that anything over 15% is excessive.[23] Would Jesus in America today seeing the impact of a 21% credit card interest rate on a family look the other way?

Efforts to cap credit card interest rates have been stopped by lobbyists. In May 2010, the credit industry killed an amendment offered by U.S. Senators Sheldon Whitehouse (D-RI) and Thad Cochran (R-MS) to the banking reform legislation.[24]

Whitehouse said that states should be allowed "to protect their residents form usurious and excessive interest rates" that "take advantage of struggling families." His amendment would have required a cap on rates based on the residency of the individual. Hence, if Delaware or South Dakota

---

[23] Michael Kranish, "Push to Curb Credit-Card Rates Fades," Boston.com, November 18, 2009. See also Joe Weisenthal, "A Case for Capping Credit Card Rates," BusinessInsider.com, April 23, 2009.

[24] The amendment would have addressed a U.S. Supreme Court ruling, *Marquette Nat. Bank v. First of Omaha Corp.*, 439 U.S. 299 (1978), that all but eliminated state usury laws. The credit card company's home base, not the residency of the consumer, was now the basis to set the interest rate.

had a very high ceiling for rates, but New York had a low one then a credit card company based in Delaware or South Dakota would have to follow New York law.[25]

The amendment had the potential to save consumers $5 billion[26]. According to Ed Mierzwinski, Consumer Program Director of U.S. Public Interest Research Group, the amendment would have enabled states to "protect their citizens from usurious actions by virtually unregulated credit card companies."[27] The amendment was defeated by a 60 to 35 vote with 5 senators not voting.[28]

---

[25] "Whitehouse Statement on Senate Vote on Marquette Amendment," May 19, 2010, Senate.gov.

[26] Caroline Dobson, "Senate Wall Street Reforms Stall Credit Card Overhaul," TheEpochTimes.com, May 20, 2010.

[27] "Is Senate Proposal Death Knell for 30% Credit-Card Rates?" Consumer Reports.org, May 19, 2010.

[28] Senators voting for the amendment to give states the power to cap credit card interest rates were:

Akaka (D-HI), Begich (D-AK), Bennet (D-CO), Boxer (D-CA), Brown (D-OH), Burris (D-IL), Cardin (D-MD), Casey (D-PA), Cochran (R-MS), Dorgan (D-ND), Durbin (D-IL), Feingold (D-WI), Feinstein (D-CA), Franken (D-MN), Gillibrand (D-NY), Harkin (D-IA), Lautenberg (D-NJ), LeMieux (R-FL), Leahy (D-VT), Levin (D-MI), McCaskill (D-MO), Merkley (D-OR), Mikulski (D-MD), Nelson (D-FL), Reed (D-RI), Reid (D-NV), Rockefeller (D-WV), Sanders (I-VT), Schumer (D-NY), Stabenow (D-MI), Udall (D-CO), Udall (D-NM), Webb (D-VA), Whitehouse (D-RI), and Wyden (D-OR).

Senators voting against the amendment to give states the power to cap credit card interest rates were:

Alexander (R-TN), Barrasso (R-WY), Baucus (D-MT), Bayh (D-IN), Bennett (R-UT), Bingaman (D-NM), Bond (R-MO), Brown (R-MA), Brownback (R-KS), Bunning (R-KY), Burr (R-NC), Cantwell (D-WA), Carper (D-DE),

Chuck Collins, co-founder of the Institute for Policy Studies, and Mary Wright of JustFaith Ministries, in *The Moral Measure of the Economy* ask – What kind of country are we becoming?[29] At this point perhaps the question may be better framed by asking – What kind of country have we become to permit interest rates that exceed 8 or 9%?[30] Is this not a call to

---

Chambliss (R-GA), Coburn (R-OK), Collins (R-ME), Conrad (D-ND), Corker (R-TN), Cornyn (R-TX), Crapo (R-ID), DeMint (R-SC), Dodd (D-CT), Ensign (R-NV), Enzi (R-WY), Graham (R-SC), Grassley (R-IA), Gregg (R-NH), Hagan (D-NC), Hatch (R-UT), Hutchison (R-TX), Inhofe (R-OK), Inouye (D-HI), Isakson (R-GA), Johanns (R-NE), Johnson (D-SD), Kaufman (D-DE), Kerry (D-MA), Klobuchar (D-MN), Kohl (D-WI), Kyl (R-AZ), Landrieu (D-LA), Lincoln (D-AR), Lugar (R-IN), McCain (R-AZ), McConnell (R-KY), Murkowski (R-AK), Murray (D-WA), Nelson (D-NE), Pryor (D-AR), Risch (R-ID), Roberts (R-KS), Sessions (R-AL), Shaheen (D-NH), Shelby (R-AL), Snowe (R-ME), Tester (D-MT), Thune (R-SD), Vitter (R-LA), Voinovich (R-OH), and Wicker (R-MS).

Not voting were: Byrd (D-WV), Lieberman (ID-CT), Menendez (D-NJ), Specter (D-PA), Warner (D-VA).

[29] Collins and Wright, *The Moral Measure of the Economy*, 59.

[30] Throughout history, especially during much of Christianity, the loaning of money with interest has been regulated, if not condemned. In addition to the Hebrew Scriptures, regulations or prohibitions existed at the time of Hammurabi's Code in 1750 B.C.; Rome's Twelve Tables in 443 B.C. at 8 1/3%; the Code of Justinian at 8 1/3% in 529 A.D.; Charlemagne outlaws usury in 800 A.D.; Medieval Canon Law made usury punishable with excommunication; Elizabeth I caps the charging of interest to no more than 10%; in 18th Century America the rate was capped at 8%; following the American Revolution most states kept it at 6%; by the early Twentieth Century usury laws were being drastically scaled back in the United States; and in 1978 the U.S. Supreme Court permits South Dakota, home to a thriving credit card industry, to impose high consumer loan rates to those outside the state. See Calvin Elliott, *Usury* (Charleston: Bibliobazaar, 2007), Willaim A.M. Visser and Alastair McIntosh, "A Short Review of the Historical Critique of Usury," *Accounting, Business & Financial History*, 8:2 July 1998, Daniel W. Matlow and Jamie B. Wasserman, "Hybrid Debt/Equity Transactions: Do They Intersect with the Usury Laws?" *Florida Bar Journal* Vol. 84 No. 4 (April 2010), and James

"cancel the debts of the oppressed; and tear apart every unjust contract" (Isaiah 58:6)?

Depending on a family or individual's income, debt with a high interest rate not paid in full each month will inevitably lead to a deeper, ongoing financial burden. Is a modern Jubilation needed to restore some level of equilibrium? Jesus sought to liberate the "oppressed" (Luke 4:18-21). Should oppressed be defined and applied differently to the working poor, middle class, or upper middle class who use credit cards?

One group may struggle less with paying off debt. Yet each is a source of profit, potentially greed or unjust gain, and those with limited income may endure harsh, unforeseen consequences. When financial burden becomes destructive does a group merit mercy, another justice, or perhaps neither since free choice has played a role? Has complacency by Christians replaced the social activism of Jesus?

Honest reflection is needed as to whether Christians, regardless of the denomination, have permitted, condoned, or legitimized inherent flaws in the existing economic framework. Have Christians failed to be their brother and sister's keeper in this area of the economy? Can an active love of God be complacent in the face of injustice?

---

M. Ackerman, "Interest Rates and the Law: A History of Usury," *Arizona State Law Journal* 61 (1981).

The Eucharist, the living embodiment of the Sermon on the Mount "effectuated by the action of the Holy Spirit,"[31] offers one model whether in the Roman, Episcopal, or Eastern Orthodox tradition to define, discuss, and potentially answer the issues that arise from the practices and especially consequences of credit bureaus, collection agencies, and credit card companies.

In some Protestant traditions where there is a different embrace of the Eucharist there is still a call to pray the Lord's Prayer. In this prayer, also a vital part of the Eastern and Western faiths, is also found an important response to consumer debt.

The Prayer and Holy Sacrifice is a reminder that everything, including personal and commercial wealth, belongs to the Creator. Every ounce of gold or pound of silver belongs to the Governor of the Universe[32] (Haggai 2:8). Eternal Life owns the earth and its fruits. The Divine Parent graciously allows humankind to benefit from God's Creation (Exodus 19:5; Leviticus 25:23; Job 41:11; Deuteronomy 10:14; 1 Chronicles 10:26, 29:11).

The Maker of All calls on every generation to be good caretakers of what they have been permitted to enjoy. This

---

[31] Sergius Bulgakov, *The Bride of the Lamb* (Grand Rapids: William B. Eerdmans Publishing, 2002), 285.

[32] Evelyn Underhill challenges the Christian sojourner to think, approach, and revere Infinite Love beyond the standard, limited, and often used word "God." This challenge is reflected here.

should carry over into the fair exchange of commercial transactions. In addition, there must be mutual, equitable benefit where one party treats the other as he or she wishes to be treated (Matthew 7:12). Fairness must be safeguarded in commercial transactions.

The Giver of Light not only lays claim to the world's wealth, but also to the debt that families and individuals struggle with everyday. In 1986, the U.S. Catholic Conference of Bishops, citing Vatican Council II, observed that "personal dignity is realized in community with others." Dignity of a sister or brother "is the criterion against which all aspects of economic life must be measured."[33]

In comparison, one evangelical approach is to "look first to our status as God's creatures" with "life properly lived in responsibility to God ..."[34] The Creator does not expect children to suffer due to the inaction of God's other children. Our place as the Almighty's Created Creation is to manifest active love for others. Are Christians in the financial sector living responsibly to God by enabling the current credit structure? Are Christians not in the financial sector, but who fail to speak out against the injustice, living responsibly to God?

---

[33] U.S. Catholic Bishops. *Pastoral Letter on Catholic Social Teaching and the U.S. Economy.* Office for Social Justice. 1986.

[34] Paul Marshall, senior fellow at the Center for Religious Freedom. See Ronald J. Sider and Diane Knippers, *Toward an Evangelical Public Policy* (Grand Rapids: BakerBooks, 2005), 312.

The Mystical Supper is one reminder to all Christians of their duty to: identify injustice, determine responsibility, assess the remedy, and take the necessary actions to restore the injured to a place had the injustice not occurred.[35] The Eucharist is the ministry of Jesus in its entirety – yesterday, today, and forever. It is infinite, timeless, universal justice that transcends anything developed by the best minds of secular society and political institutions. The Eucharist is the mission of the collective Christian church in action.[36]

---

[35] Howard Zehr in *The Little Book of Restorative Justice* (Intercourse, PA: Good Books, 2002) outlines five guiding questions of restorative justice: "Who has been hurt? What are their needs? Whose obligations are these? Who has a stake in this situation? What is the appropriate process to involve stakeholders in an effort to put things right?" 38. Although Zehr's focus is toward the criminal justice system, his overall ethical model also has relevance on economic justice.

[36] Daniel B . Clendenin, ed. *Eastern Orthodox Theology – A Contemporary Reader* (Grand Rapids: Baker Books, 1995), 200.

# Sacralization and Commoditization

American religious culture has made certain allowances for the free market system. This may stem from "sacralizing" or making sacred the nation's secular economic system. It's not likely that the Holy One blessed unbridled capitalism where survival of the fittest is supreme.[37]

Faith and religion has been Americanized leading it to apply a false-sacredness to behaviors, attitudes, and principles in politics and business that attempt to give it an endorsement on God's behalf. The need to place the American flag in a house of worship at the very front, as an example, is symbolic of the all too close relationship of faith and civic duty.

According to Max L. Stackhouse, "theological and ethical assessments of economic life have largely accepted secular, materialist and political views of our past." He adds that this has skewed morality.[38] Christians are immersed in a culture

---

[37] Vigen Guroian, *Incarnate Love – Essays in Orthodox Ethics* (Notre Dame: University of Notre Dame Press, 2002), 172. Guroian observes that Protestant fundamentalism "sacralizes" both American politics regardless of its problem and capitalist economy being unable to offer a genuine Christian critique of some of the social problems confronting the country. In general, Guroian and others ask if Orthodoxy can achieve the same result without becoming "Americanized" thus losing its moral compass. The causes, however, for sacralized secularism can be traced to Emperor Constantine. See Alexander Men, *Christianity for the Twenty-First Century* (New York: Continuum, 1996), 121-126.

[38] Robin Gill, ed. *The Cambridge Companion to Christian Ethics* (Cambridge: Cambridge University Press, 2008), 228.

that lulls them to insensitivity or complacency about this aspect of economic injustice that impacts their ethical and spiritual objectivity. It distorts their moral outlook that contributes to the excesses of consumerism. Something sacred like faith is being used to enable bad behavior or unethical business practices not unlike taking a place of prayer and turning it into a "den of thieves" (Matthew 21:12-13).

An example of sacralized secularism is evidenced among some evangelical Protestants in the promotion of the "prosperity gospel." In August 2009, Gloria Copeland told a crowd of about 9,000 at a prosperity gospel service that "God knows where the money is, and he knows how to get the money to you."

According to *New York Times* reporter Laurie Goodstein, "preachers delighted the crowd with anecdotes about the luxurious lives they had attained by following the Word of God." This included boats, private airplanes, designer handbags, bejeweled rings, and trips to Hawaii. The Copelands have 386,000 regular donors to their ministry. A guest preacher at the event told "God's elect" that while "everybody else is having a famine [God's] covenant people will be having the best of times."[39]

---

[39] Laurie Goodstein, "Believers Invest in the Gospel of Getting Rich," *New York Times*, August 16, 2009.

Bishop Eddie Long of the New Birth Missionary Baptist Church has justified his million dollar salary, $1.4 million home, and $350,000 Bentley due to the burden of running "an international corporation." He told the *Atlanta Journal-Constitution* that he deals with world leaders. "We're not just a bumbling bunch of preachers ... You've got to put me on a different scale than the little black preacher sitting over there that's supposed to be just getting by because the people are suffering."[40]

In an interview with AOL News, Julian Bond, former leader of the NAACP, called Long a "prosperity minister" who preaches about getting rich, not salvation. He referred to Long as "extravagantly paid."[41]

America is a status-driven nation where the value of an individual's personhood is often measured by his or her titles, wealth, clothes, degrees, and even the car driven. This has been allowed to impact personal faith and religion. Citizens have been conditioned to think that living the dream – the American Dream – is about home ownership and material success. This mindset manifested in part through the prosperity gospel, existed long before Rev. Ike, one of its founders back in the 1970's. He

---

[40] Larry Hartstein, "Bishop Eddie Long – Megachurch had Modest Beginning," AJC.com, September 23, 2010.

[41] Mara Gay, "Before Sex Scandal, Bishop Long Built an Empire," AOLNews.com, September 24, 2010.

did, however, tirelessly promote it and disagreed with Apostle Paul that money was the "root of all evil."[42]

Former Southern Baptist Convention president Jimmy Allen told a gathering of African-American Baptists that the prosperity gospel "is now a problem because we've learned to study the market, and now the marketplace is dictating the message."[43]

According to Prof. Ronald J. Sider, Director of the Sider Center on Ministry and Public Policy at Eastern Baptist Theological Seminary, evangelicals have chosen to "spend more and more on themselves and give a smaller and smaller percentage to the church." Sider refers to a "cultural setting that absolutizes" consumerism among evangelicals.[44]

In discussing pay day lending, Christopher Peterson co-author of a 2008 study observed that a "generation ago, populist Christian leaders were among the most aggressive opponents of usurious lending. But today many Christian leaders take large

---

[42] Christopher Lehmann-Haupt, "Reverend Ike, Who Preached Riches, Dies at 74," NYTimes.com, July 30, 2009.

[43] Hannah Elliott, "National Baptist Speakers Criticize Prosperity Gospel, 'Seeker' Churches," AMPNews.com, September 8, 2006.

[44] Ronald J. Sider, *The Scandal of the Evangelical Conscience* (Grand Rapids: BakerBooks, 2005), 20-21 and 115.

campaign contributions from the credit industry and no longer support the Biblical injunction against usury."[45]

Rebecca Todd Peters points to the capitalist-driven "Contract with America" of the early 1990s which "offers an excellent example of a very particularized theological ideology that was touted as representing the 'Christian' point of view."[46] She further noted that values and faith have become "commodified" or made into a product due in part to an insatiable consumerism that dominates every aspect of culture.[47] There are obvious similarities between this and the conduct in the temple that made Jesus angry.

In July 2009, this commoditization likely contributed to record level credit card delinquencies. According to the American Bankers Association, delinquencies were the highest since it first began tracking such data in 1974.[48] Between 2005 and 2007, collection companies received about $40 billion a year.

---

[45] Stephanie Mencimer, "Christians Heart Payday Lenders," MotherJones.com, March 5, 2008 and Steven M. Graves and Christopher L. Peterson, "Usury Law and the Christian Right: Faith-Based Political Power and the Geography of American Payday Loan Regulation," 57 *Catholic University Law Review* 637, Spring 2008.

[46] Peters. *In Search of the Good Life* (New York: The Continuum International Publishing Group, 2004), 20.

[47] Ibid., 151.

[48] "Credit Card Delinquencies at Record High," MSNBC.com, July 7, 2009.

One out four complaints to the Federal Trade Commission concerns debt collectors.[49]

It should be remembered that the economy has a cyclical nature. Politicians, public servants, and policy makers have yet to figure out a means to limit or neutralize the inevitable economic sting that will hit in the future. Even during a strong economic period, however, fewer people may be unemployed yet the weight of debt will remain a heavy burden for millions.

Although highly visible, the prosperity gospel or the Contract with America is hardly the primary contributing factors to making sacred an economic system whose excesses contribute to financial hardship. There are few, if any, Christian organizations, which don't take donations or enable purchases of Bibles, icons, statues, and prayer ropes, among other things, using credit cards. These organizations are enablers.

In 2007, the Catholic Archdiocese of Cincinnati became the first such diocese that permitted parishioners to donate using credit cards.[50] During Christmas 2008, the Salvation Army started taking donations at street corner red kettles with debit and credit cards.[51]

---

[49] Linda Stern, "A New Shakedown?" Newsweek.com, July 21, 2008.

[50] Karen Vance, "Archdiocese Passes Online Plate," New.Enquirer.com, December 24, 2007.

[51] "Salvation Army Kettles Now Take Plastic," MSNBC.com, November 25, 2009.

Tax and regulatory allowances for Christian organizations of all denominations has likely further contributed to creating a myth that America's capitalist economy is sacred and divinely sanctioned. Faith groups are now running everything from fitness clubs to ice cream parlors with tax and zoning advantages not available to businesses or other nonprofits.[52]

Perhaps it was an early form of making faith and values a product or commodity as well as the defilement of the holy temple that made Jesus drive out those who bought and sold in the temple (Mark 11:15-17). Christian leaders and their flocks must take some level of responsibility for the current environment that allows the current practices of the credit card, credit bureau, and collection agency sectors.

According to theologian William Barclay, Satan's offer to give Jesus all the world's kingdoms (Matthew 4:8-9) was "all the more acute because of the dreams of prosperity and plenty" that were to accompany the "messianic age."[53] Jesus rejected the lure of wealth and material gain. Clearly, the spiritual

---

[52] Diana b. Henriques, "As Exemptions Grow, Religion Outweighs Regulations," NYTimes.com, October 8, 2006 and Henriques; "As Religious Programs Expand, Disputes Rise Over Tax Breaks," NYTimes.com, October 10, 2006; and Henriques, "Where Faith Abides, Employees Have Few Rights," NYTimes.com, October 9, 2006.

[53] William Barclay, "The Mind of Jesus" (New York: Harper-Collins, 1976), 38.

distractions during the time of Jesus have remained an ongoing challenge in modern "Christian" America. In fact, they remain unchanged.

These distractions remain despite the gift and constant presence of the Eucharist. The Mystical Supper has become a routine to acknowledge, not love God. Its relational nature has been marginalized thus distancing the individual from the Creator and causing division within the Christian family. Its holy call to mission has been diminished as evidenced by the inaction or widespread acceptance of legally permitted activities that cause spiritual, emotional, and physical harm. The Eucharist is ever present to help the faithful to reclaim the Christian values that have become overlooked or forgotten, especially in an age of rampant, tolerated financial exploitation.

Christians have contributed to the secularization of America and the marginalization of their own faith by inaction toward unjust gain and predatory consumer lending.[54] Increasingly Christianity is becoming a label, process, and ritual bordering on superstition, not a dynamic faith of action, activism, and advocacy demonstrating active love for humankind and the living Jesus in each of us.

---

[54] Paul Peter Jesep, "Crucifying Jesus and Secularizing America – the Republic of Faith Without Wisdom" (Xlibris: 2008).

# Social Impact

*Consequences*

Giving moral legitimacy to capitalism probably contributed to scaling back America's bankruptcy laws. At one time bankruptcy laws permitted a family or individual a fresh start. In 2005, the banking and credit card industries successfully lobbied Congress to limit the option.[55]

This occurred despite the circumstances that drove most Americans to pursue the discharge of debt. According to the National Association of Consumer Bankruptcy Attorneys, seventy-nine percent of those in heavy debt was "caused by circumstances beyond their control." These circumstances included divorce, job loss, medical expenses, and family death. Only twenty-one percent were identified as those in debt due to "circumstances within their control."[56]

The report further noted that under the 2005 bankruptcy reform, "fewer than one out of 20 consumers (3.3 percent) were candidates for paying off what they owe under a

---

[55] Molly Ivins, "Bad to Worse," WorkingForChange.com, March 3, 2005.

[56] National Association of Consumer Bankruptcy Attorneys, "Bankruptcy Reform's Impact: Where Are All the Deadbeats," February 22, 2006. A study by Prof. John a. E. Pottow of the University of Michigan has found that two-thirds of senior citizens filing for bankruptcy do so because of credit card debt. See Janet Novack, "Credit Card Debt Blamed for Surge in Elder Bankruptcy," Forbes.com, October 12, 2010.

debt management plan, with the remaining 96.7 percent requiring the same bankruptcy filing that they would have needed before the new bankruptcy law went into effect."[57]

Before the bankruptcy reform "the number of bankruptcy filings – even at its pinnacle – represents only a sliver of those struggling with bills."[58] The banking lobby successfully used shame as a moral argument to restrict bankruptcy. "Proponents spent much less time discussing the economics of the consumer credit industry."[59]

Prof. Elizabeth Warren noted in a *Newsweek* interview that "This is one of those times when the imbalance in lobbying could not have been more grotesque." She said that the law delays the bankruptcy process through mandatory counseling "so that people would make payments for another three to six months" before seeing a lawyer. According to her and confirming the findings of the National Association of Consumer Bankruptcy Attorneys, "Ninety percent of the

---

[57] Ibid.

[58] Ronald J. Mann and Katherine Porter, *Saving Up for Bankruptcy*, 98 Georgetown Law Journal 289 (2010).

[59] Ronald J. Mann, *Bankruptcy Reform and the 'Sweat box' of Credit Card Debt*," 376 University of Illinois Law Review Vol. 2007.

families who file for bankruptcy do so following a job loss, a medical problem or a family torn apart by death or divorce."[60]

U.S. Senator Mitch McConnell (R-KY), a spirited advocate of limiting bankruptcy access, said that the new law "ushered in a new emphasis on personal responsibility." The Kentucky Senator received $4.3 million in campaign donations from the banking industry.

Travis Plunkett, legislative director for the Consumer Federation of America, said that "I've been at this work [advocacy for good government] for close to 20 years. I've never seen a lobby in Washington as powerful as banking and financial services"[61] According to the Center for Responsive

---

[60] Karen Springen, "Going for Broke," MSNBC.com, August 31, 2006. See in general Teresa A. Sullivan, *The Fragile Middle Class* (New Haven: Yale University Press, 2000).

[61] See John Cheves, "Critics: Reform Backed by McConnell Fostered Crisis," Kentucky.com, October 2, 2008. Between 1989 and 2005, bank lobbyists pushing the bankruptcy reform bill that McConnell championed donated $40 million to members of Congress. See "Career Profiles Show Lawmakers' 16 Year Fundraising Totals," OpenSecrets.org., March 8, 2005.

See in general, Amy Buttell Crane, "Bankruptcy Law Another blow for Katrina Victims," BankRate.com, September 2005 and Peralte C. Paul, "Katrina Victims Unlikely to Get Break on New Bankruptcy Law," September 22, 2005, AJC.com, Travis Plunkett, legislative director for the Consumer Federation of America, said that "I've been at this work [advocacy for good government] for close to 20 years. I've never seen a lobby in Washington as powerful as banking and financial services" See Paul Peter Jesep, "Stop Financial Vampirsim," *Portsmouth Herald*, October 19, 2001.

In April 2010, after meeting with Wall Street executives McConnell came out strongly opposed to a Democratic proposal that would overhaul the financial industry. McConnell said that it would force taxpayers to bailout failing banks. See Rachel Martin, "President Obama Criticizes Mitch McConnell in Finance

Politics, among the ten largest campaign donors between 1989 and 2010 in Congressional elections were Morgan Stanley, JP Morgan, and Goldman Sachs.[62]

Not long after passage of the bankruptcy overhaul the Katrina hurricane devastated Louisiana and badly damaged Florida, Alabama, and Mississippi. Congress refused to make allowances in the draconian new bankruptcy law for citizens who were financially devastated by the storm.

Independent of debt, interest, and bankruptcy there remains an often overlooked area that has a very large impact on the financial health of average Americans. Credit bureaus have been empowered to collect large amounts of data on individuals that are used to pre-qualify many for goods and services. They determine a numeric score for each person seeking credit.

Bureaus are not bound to conduct thorough investigations when a credit report is disputed. Bureaus confirm the accuracy of information that is provided by a collection agency or credit card company, not that it is accurate. Yet low credit scores can cause higher mortgages, auto loan rates, and car insurance costs. Rental applications can be rejected, utilities can require an upfront deposit, and cell phone companies are not likely to offer equally good deals given to other customers. An

---

Reform Push," April 17, 2010, ABCNews.com. See also Sheryl Gay Stolberg, "Obama Vows to Move on Regulation," April 17, 2010, NYTimes.com.

[62] Bruce Watson, "The 10 Biggest Corporate Campaign Contributors in U.S. Politics," DailyFinance.com, October 13, 2010.

individual or family can even be denied a student loan due to a weak score.[63]

In addition, the information provided to a potential landlord or employer, for example, is different than what the person most impacted sees. He or she is not entitled to review what is given out. Time spent in a drug rehabilitation clinic can easily show up on the report, but credit bureaus give assurances that it would never be seen. This does not include data entry people at the credit bureaus who will review part of your personal life.[64]

Evan Hendricks, author of "Credit Scores & Credit Reports: How the System Really Works, What You Can Do," told the *Christian Science Monitor* that credit scores are a "civil rights issue because of the growing use of credit reports and credit scores for hiring, renting an apartment, insurance, and the fact that people of color have not been integrated into the credit scoring system as much as traditional, white, middle-class America." In 2007, thirty-five percent of employers used credit scores to assess a candidate's qualifications.[65]

---

[63] Julie Sturgeon, "Bad Credit Hurts in Many Ways," Bankrate.com, June 16, 2008.

[64] Bob Sullivan, "The Red Tape Chronicles – Are Clinic Visits on Credit Reports?" MSNBC.com, May 9, 2006.

[65] Ben Arnoldy, "The Spread of the Credit Check as Civil Rights Issue – Minorities are Starting to Fight Employers Over the Use of Credit History in Hiring," CSMonitor.com, January 18, 2007.

This is larger than civil rights. It is better described as human rights issue since it includes civil, political, and economic concerns.[66] Being unable to secure a job or safe, clean housing coupled with the powerlessness, due to the influence of special interest money in Washington, to provide a level of fairness and equity raises issues that go beyond civil rights.

Several states have attempted to ban the practice of using a credit score in evaluating a job applicant. According to attorney Merle Turchik, "A lot of times [a credit score] can be irrelevant to the job that you're looking to be hired for." [67]

According to some employment attorneys there "is no evidence that supports the idea that an applicant's credit history is reflective of a person's propensity to steal or their suitability for employment …"[68] In a survey of 100 employers by the Society of Human Resource Management 60% of respondents used credit histories to determine employment suitability. So far the Credit Bureau industry has successfully lobbied at both the state and federal level to stop legislation to limit or regulate use of scores.[69] Limiting use of scores could limit their profit.

---

[66] U.S. Catholic Bishops. *Pastoral Letter on Catholic Social Teaching and the U.S. Economy.* Office for Social Justice. 1986.

[67] Sergio Avila, "Can Your Credit Score Cost You a Job? 9OYS Investigates," KGUN9.com, May 21, 2010.

[68] John W. Schoen, "Bad Credit Sidelines some Jobless Workers," MSNBC.com, February 23, 2010.

[69] Ibid.

A consumer who has always made timely payments beyond the minimum can receive a reduced credit score if a credit card company scales back a credit line. Mark Huffman of ConsumerAffairs.com writes that when a "credit card company lowers your credit line, it has a negative affect on your credit score. You have less credit available to you and, if your carry balances on your cards, the ratio of debt to available credit rises sharply."[70]

"Responsible behavior" also can hurt the arbitrary credit score that consumers are assigned and have limited ability to challenge. According to Jeffrey Weber, a blogger for SmartBalanceTransfers.com, "If all of a sudden you go from using 35% or 40% of your available credit to 90% [due to reducing a credit line], that's going to have a huge effect on your credit score." According to Weber, the "card companies' computerized models are being counterintuitive. These people are paying down their debt and then their limits are reduced even though they're trying to avoid delinquency."[71]

In addition, "If you cancel your card you will reduce your fees, but it can adversely affect your credit score," according to Margaret O'Meara, a certified financial planner. "If

---

[70] Mark Huffman, "CARD Act Could Impact Your Credit Score," ConsumerAffairs.com, March 22, 2010.

[71] Asher Hawkins, "Credit Card Customers Punished for Doing the Right Thing?" ABCNews.com, April 11, 2010.

you close the card, this will be a credit limit reduction and will affect your credit utilization measure. About one third of your credit score is based on how much credit you are actually using."[72]

A credit consultant referred to a person's score as a "grown up report card."[73] It's an odd description considering that Wall Street barons who contributed to the financial collapse through questionable business tactics all are likely to have had sterling credit scores.

In 2008, Congress officially authorized a bank bailout of $700 billion. In 2009, actual taxpayer commitments exceeded several trillion dollars.[74] Keep in mind that taxpayers helping with the bailout include those with credit cards with very high interest rates.

Credit scores are largely determined by a computer-generated formula by Fair, Isaac and Company (FICO), a corporation traded on the New York Stock Exchange. The corporation, started by Bill Fair, an engineer, and Earl Isaac, a mathematician, in 1956, provides the information to credit bureaus. An individual's worth as a human being is determined

---

[72] Karin Price Mueller, "Assessment Needed Before Canceling a Credit Card," DelawareOnline.com, April 17, 2010.

[73] Avila, "Can Your Credit Score Cost You a Job? 9OYS Investigates."

[74] Andy Kroll, "Bank Bailout: The Greatest Swindle Ever Sold," Salon.com, May 27, 2009.

by a mathematical formula. In April 2010, it was reported that 25.5 percent of consumers had poor FICO scores. "In normal times," wrote one business writer the number is about 15 percent.[75] In July 2010, 43.4 million Americans had credit scores of 599 or below.[76]

Even if the 15 percent figure "in normal times" is used as a starting point for discussion there are millions of people denied their personhood. Unemployment, medical problems, or perhaps a devastating fire that destroyed a person's home are not factored in. In 2010, a national unemployment rate just under 10 percent is considered unacceptable. Clearly, allowing this percentage of consumers to be harmed due to a computer formula is equally unacceptable.

Maintaining a good FICO score is a game. Paying all your bills in a timely manner doesn't necessarily give you a high or higher score. Nor will making timely payments to a collection agency help. Opening a new account, even if you close another, can hurt your score.[77] Attorney and consumer advocate Leonard Bennett testified before Congress that the "ability to predict risk

---

[75] Laurent Belsie, "Credit Scores Slide Downward," CSMonitor.com, July 27, 2010.

[76] "FICO Scores Sink to a New Low for Americans: Morgan Drexen Asks Are FICO Scores Realistic?" PRWeb.com, July 22, 2010.

[77] Martha C. White, "Good Credit Score Secrets," WalletPop.com, July 7, 2010.

and integrate that into a credit score – based on historic data – is logically impossible."[78]

Once a score is deemed poor it can take five or six years to improve. In addition, some question the accuracy of FICO scores. It was FICO scores that overextended credit to many which contributed to Wall Street's financial melt down. In an informal survey of attorney's who are retained by those struggling financially, there are "many" "who have high FICO scores but still need help managing their rising debt" through legal counsel.[79]

It has been estimated that a poor credit score costs the consumer $201,712 in a lifetime.[80] Congress has failed to reign in FICO, "the leading provider of analytics and decision management technology."[81] It appears that the oil industry has more oversight than many financial services.

A 2009 report issued by New York State Attorney General Andrew Cuomo noted, "when banks did well, their employees were paid well. When the banks did poorly, their employees were paid well." Cuomo said that "when the banks

---

[78] Kathy Chu and Sandra Block, "As Lenders Clamp Down, Credit Scores Take a Hit," USAToday.com, September 23, 2009.

[79] Ibid.

[80] MSN Money Staff, "Your 5-Minute Guide to Credit Scores," MoneyCentral.MSN.com, March 18, 2010.

[81] "Sam's Club Deploys FICO Retail Action Manager to Boost Member Loyalty," FICO.com, June 3, 2010.

did very poorly, they were bailed out by taxpayers and their employees were still paid well. Bonuses and overall compensation did not vary significantly as profits diminished."[82]

In analyzing 2008 bonuses, Cuomo's report documented that Troubled Asset Relief Program (TARP) recipients like Citigroup and Merrill Lynch lost a combined $54 billion, but paid out $9 billion in bonuses while taking a total of $55 billion in bailout money, funded in part by banks like Citigroup.[83]

The report also revealed that 2008 bonuses for Goldman Sachs, Morgan Stanley, and J.P. Morgan Chase "were substantially greater than the banks' net income." In total, these institutions earned $9.6 billion, paid bonuses of nearly $18 billion and received TARP taxpayer funs worth $45 billion."[84]

High FICO scores would not have made a difference among the top executives at Goldman Sachs in projecting job performance. In April 2010, the Securities and Exchange Commission filed a civil lawsuit against the firm accusing it of defrauding its customers.[85] A month later the New York State Attorney General initiated an investigation into some of Wall

---

[82] New York State Attorney General's Office, "No Rhyme or Reasons: The 'Heads I Win, Tails You Lose' Bank Bonus Culture," July 30, 2009.

[83] Ibid.

[84] Ibid.

[85] Louise Story and Gretchen Morgenson, "For Goldman, a Bet's Stakes Keep Growing," NYTimes.com, April 17, 2010.

Street's most prestigious institutions alleging that they knowingly provided false information to credit rating agencies that contributed to the financial collapse.[86]

Oxfam International reported that the trillions of dollars the Group of Twenty Finance Ministers and Central Bank Governors (G20) of the world's biggest economies gave in bank bailout money would be "enough to end global extreme poverty for 50 years and a massive step towards ending it forever ..."[87]

Chi Chi Wu, a staff attorney for the nonprofit National Consumer Law Center, called the use of credit checks "harmful and unfair to American workers." U.S. Senator Dianne Feinstein (CA-D) and U.S. Representative Steve Cohen (TN-D) have both introduced legislation to ban the use of credit scores in the hiring of personnel.[88] The Equal Employment Act (H.R. 3149) has languished in committee since July 2009.

Delinquencies, credit card debt, and poor credit scores contribute to divorce, suicide[89], anxiety, insomnia, debilitating

---

[86] "Wall Street Faces N.Y. Probe on Ratings Data," Money.CNN.com, May 13, 2010.

[87] "Bank Bailout Could End Poverty for 50 Years – Oxfam Tells G20," Press Release, Oxfam.org, April 1, 2009.

[88] Margaret Collins, "Credit History for Insurance, Hiring Eyed by Congress," BusinessWeek.com, May 23, 2010. See also Sara Murray, "Employer Credit Checks on Job Seekers Draw Scrutiny," WSJ.com, October 21, 2010.

[89] See Alice Gomstyn, "Did Debt Collection Calls Kill this Man?" ABCNews.com, September 22, 2009 and Rich Phillips, "Woman Sues Debt Collector Over Husband's Death," CNN.com, December 10, 2009.

headaches, stomach disorders, and high blood pressure. According to Dr. Alan Manevitz, a clinical psychiatrist at New York-Presbyterian/Weill Cornel Medical Center in Manhattan, debt has created a new medical condition called Debt Stress Syndrome (DSS).[90]

Paul J. Lavrakas, a research psychologist, observed that 10 to 16 million Americans are "suffering terribly due to their debts . . ." According to Dr. Lavrakas, persons reporting debt stress complain of ulcers, migraines, heart attacks, and severe depression.[91] DSS also can lead to drug and alcohol abuse and eating disorders.[92] Further research is needed on the likely impact DSS has on interpersonal relationships both at home and in the work place.[93]

Recent surveys, however, show that debt is among the top reasons for divorce.[94] Pope Benedict XVI has repeatedly sounded the alarm that marriage is under threat due to societal

---

[90] "Coping with 'Debt Stress Syndrome," CBSNews.com, June 14, 2008.

[91] "Poll: Stress of Debt Takes Physical Toll," CNN.com, June 8, 2008.

[92] Kelly McGonigal, "Debt and Stress," WashingtonPost.com, July 24, 2007.

[93] Tom Gilbert, "A Fate Worse than Debt: Credit Cards and Stress," TheDoctorWillSeeYouNow.com, Printed August 30, 2008.

[94] See in general, Eileen A J Connelly, "How Money Can Impact a Marriage (Associated Press), MainStreet.com, July 22, 2009; Tom Grant "Bad Money Habits Can Cause a Marriage to Fail" (*Pittsburgh Post-Gazette*) ReporterNews.com, June 13, 2009; and "Credit Card Debt May Be Leading Cause of Divorce," PRLog.org, April 6, 2008.

excesses. Clearly, consumer debt should be high on the list of problems that actually threatens marriage.

"Financial stress can negatively – even severely – impact things outside of the wallet: your health, your job, and your relationships," confirmed David Alecock, a vice president at InCharge Institute, a nonprofit credit counseling organization.[95] Ted Hagen, PhD, a family psychologist and authors Judi Light Hopson and Emma H. Hopson, R.N. of *Burnout to Balance: EMS Stress* cited in an op-ed a debt counselor who described some seeking help as so anxious that they were exploring death as an option. The counselor also concluded, as have other experts, that credit card debt is destroying families and friendships.[96]

Daniel J. Reidenberg with Suicide Awareness Voices of Education (SAVE) said that illness, job loss, and family pressure contribute to depression. Financial pressures in particular can put someone "over the edge" and lead the person to suicide.[97] In one case, a Discover Card representative told a delinquent debtor that she faced jail time and that contact had already been

---

[95] Emily Starbuck Gerson, "Severe Debt Can Cause Depression and Even Suicide," CreditCards.com., September 8, 2008.

[96] Judi Light Hopson, Emma H.. Hopson, R.N., and Ted Hagen, Ph.D, "Credit Card Debt Can Wreck Relationships," SeattleTimes.com, May 17, 2010.

[97] Ibid.

made with a local prosecutor. It drove her to suicide.[98] Economic despair has been a major contributor to an 18% increase in persons seeking help through suicide prevention centers in 2010.[99]

Consumer finance analyst Laura Nishikawa noted of one major credit card company that it uses a business approach based on "penalty pricing." The company depends on high fees for missed payments and raising interest rates when a limit is exceeded.[100] Hence, a marketing strategy is developed around this expectation.

Two former employees of MBNA charged that the credit card giant had an internal policy to get customers to max out their credit cards. Jim Campen, director of the Americans for Fairness in Lending, said that "We haven't identified any illegal practices. What we've seen are practices that are highly unethical. It's extraordinarily common."[101]

Capital One garnished the wages of a former cardholder who attempted to make ends meet with a retail job, having lost

---

[98] "Discover's Debt Collectors' Threats Drive Woman to Suicide," Consumerist.com, June 8, 2007.

[99] Scott Martelle, "Amid Lack of Jobs, Suicide Hot Line Calls Surge," AOLNews.com, July 6, 2010.

[100] Jennifer Waters, "Another Shoe to Drop – Bad credit-Card Debt Could be Next Shot to Economy, Research Says," MarketWatch.com, September 30, 2008.

[101] Deborah Feyerick, "Ex-Bankers On Pushing Customers to Rack Up Debt," CNN.com, September 25, 2008.

her primary employment, by garnishing 25 percent of her wages. These court awards are often provided absent the debtor and the creditor showing proof that the money is owed. In some cases the creditor wins by default when a debtor fails to respond to a summons.[102] In light of the physical and emotional impact on the debtor noted above it isn't surprising that many are too traumatized to show up in court, assuming they've received notice.

In another case, Beneficial won a default judgment of $4,750. This did not include $900 in lawyer fees. Interest was assessed at 27.55 percent. Wages were garnished. After six years Beneficial received $10,000 and the debtor still owed $3,965. According to a consumer lawyer who eventually took on the case pro bono, "It's a perfectly legal result under Virginia law."[103]

An attorney with Atlanta Legal Aid observed that the working poor "have difficulties maintaining payments on life's necessities with their full paycheck. You lose 25 percent of it and everything folds."[104]

Most Americans won't discuss or acknowledge credit card debt. Citizens would rather talk about religion than personal debt. Citing a poll conducted by GfK Roper Public

---

[102] John Collins Rudolf. "Pay Garnishments Rise as Debtors Fall Behind," NYTimes.com, 1 April 2010.

[103] Ibid.

[104] Ibid.

Affairs and Media, business writer Connie Prater asked rhetorically, "How can [Americans] begin to solve their credit card debt problems if they aren't willing to face the facts and talk about their predicaments?"[105]

Pride is perhaps one of the greatest obstacles to reform. This may explain why 10-16 million Americans who suffer from debt related stress have not mobilized. Americans have become conditioned through "extreme individualism" to think that if you can't succeed in the land of plenty then it is your fault. Success in what is often described as a Judeo-Christian country is not determined by the efforts to live a Christian life, but rather by material and professional gain.[106] It contributes to false and secularized faith.[107]

In 2009, Congress passed the Credit Card Accountability, Responsibility and Disclosure Act (CARD Act) to better regulate the credit card industry. One important component of the 2009 law is that it shields young adults, especially college students, who have little or no income.

---

[105] Connie Prater, "Poll: Credit Card Debt the New Taboo Topic," CreditCards.com, July 1, 2008.

[106] See Collins & Wright, *The Moral Measure of the Economy*, 28, 83-84, 160, & 173.

[107] See Jesep, "Crucifying Jesus and Secularizing America – the Republic of Faith without Wisdom."

Parents will have to co-sign a credit card application.[108] Loopholes to snag students are already being used.[109]

Other provisions to the CARD Act include: oversight and regulations from the Federal Reserve Board; credit card companies can only increase fees, interest rates, and finance charges in certain cases; the consumer must agree that a fee will be charged if the credit limit is exceeded; and fees, penalties, and charges must reflect and be in proportion to the violation. Federal regulators will now be empowered to determine if interest rates were based on where a person shops.[110]

Unfortunately and most important, there is nothing to cap and bring down high credit card interest rates. In addition, the industry is finding ways around the law prompting the president of Southern Vermont College to editorialize that consumers "still need to be vigilant with respect to their credit

---

[108] Yet it appears that the law's impact has yet to be felt. See Christie Roshau "Credit Card Reform Law's Impact on Campus: 'What Law?'" CreditCards.com, May 11, 2010. Questions are already being raised whether the banks will abide by the law.

[109] The latest gimmick is a plastic card not covered by the new law that enables students "easier" access, for a price, to their education loans. Students are already complaining about inactivity fees, ATM charges, costs for using a PIN for a purchase instead of a signature, and in some cases their mandatory use as a campus ID card. See Ylan Q. Mui, "The New Couple on Campus: Student Loan and Debit Card," WashingtonPost.com, October 4, 2010.

[110] See in General "Fact Sheet: Reforms to Protect American Credit Card Holders," Press Release, WhiteHouse.gov, May 22, 2009 and Gerri Detweiler, "Understanding the Credit Card Accountability Responsibility and Disclosure Act of 2009," Credit.com, June 2009.

cards . . . consumers still can and will be taken advantage of in the consumer financial markets."[111]

Connecticut Attorney General Richard Blumenthal sent a letter to the Federal Reserve Board noting that it chose "to protect the interests of Wall Street bankers at the expense of Main Street consumers – putting concerns for bank safety and soundness ahead of consumer protection." He added that the Board's "apparent favoritism of banks mocks the clear Congressional intent evidenced in the CARD Act to protect consumers from the abuses of credit card issues and underscores the need for a strong, independent Consumer Financial Protection Agency that puts consumers first." He further wrote that "proposed regulations do not actually require interest rate reductions regardless of how unjustified the increase."[112]

After the CARD Act passed there was a "shameful frenzy of credit card interest rate spikes [that] saddled millions of Americans with high cost debt, including many consumers who always paid their bills on time," according to Lauren Bowne, counsel with Consumers Union. She added that the "Fed should undo that damage by requiring banks to lower interest

---

[111] Karen Gross, "Credit Card Companies Won't Quit," TimesUnion.com, 21 March 2010.

[112] "Conn. Attorney General Wants Credit Card Rates Rolled Back," ConsumerAffairs.com, April 14, 2010.

rates for customers who were treated unfairly before the new credit card protections went into effect."[113]

Other loopholes that exist pertain to "corporate" or "professional" cards that employees use on business. American Express, the largest issuer of such cards, need not obey the CARD Act. As reported by Bob Sullivan, according to Synovate, a tracker of credit card solicitations, there has been a 250 percent increase in such mailings.[114] The intent is clear – circumvent the law. It may have a dramatic, negative impact on small businesses.

In 2010, Congress passed the Consumer Financial Protection Act. Its focus is to prevent irresponsible financial practices that caused Wall Street's meltdown. It also created the Consumer Financial Protection Bureau. The Bureau's ability to monitor and successfully propose legislative reforms are yet to be tested.[115] Consumer groups have already raised concerns that it doesn't have enough strength to protect card users.

---

[113] James Limbach, "Consumers Union Urges Rollback of Recent Credit Card Interest Rate Hikes," ConsumerAffairs.com, April 16, 2010.

[114] Bob Sullivan, "What's In Your Wallet?" RedTape.MSNBC.com, September 7, 2010. See also Jessica Silver-Greenberg, "The New Credit-Card Tricks," WSJ.com, July 31, 2010.

[115] See Bob Sullivan, "The New Consumer Agency: What's in it for You," RedTape.MSNBC.com, July 21, 2010; Jim Puzzanghera, "House, Senate Lawmakers Reach a Deal on financial Reform," LATimes.com, June 25, 2010; and Ron Lieber and Tara Siegel Bernard, "From Card Fees to Mortgages, a New Day for Consumers," NYTimes.com, June 25, 2010.

Independent of the 2009 and 2010 Acts is the Fair Debt Collection Practices Act.[116] This Act still allows modest damages in most cases[117] against collection agencies who: use harassment and verbal abuse; threaten a law suit when it is not likely to happen; report old debt to credit bureaus after the statute of limitations has tolled, disclose embarrassing information to third parties such as a boss or relative; and attempt to collect on amounts that are not authorized by the agreement that created the credit card obligation.

Although there is potential for emotional distress as actual damages, statutory damages are a maximum $1,000 in most cases.[118] Consumer rights lawyers take these cases because attorney fees and costs are recoverable. Hence the client need not provide a retainer. It is more cost-effective for a collection agency to be sued multiple times than to change the practices it has in place.

In one case, a debt collector told a ten year Florida girl that her father would be arrested. The child was told "you better

---

[116] Section 801 of title VIII of the Act of May 29, 1968 (Pub. L. No. 90--321), as added by the Act of September 20, 1977 (Pub. L. No. 95--109; 91 Stat. 874), effective March 20, 1978.

[117] Michelle Ruiz, "Vile Voice Mails Cost Agency $1.5 Million," AOLNews.com, June 2, 2010. A Texas jury awarded a record $1.5 million against the racial tactics using expletives against a Lewisville man. So far this is the exception to the rule.

[118] In very rare cases, courts have awarded significantly more. See Ruiz, "Vile Voice Mails Cost Agency $1.5 Million," AOLNews.com, June 2, 2010.

kiss your daddy goodbye. He's going to be arrested tomorrow or the next day." Not more than a $1,000 was expected in a successful law suit by the father.[119]

One attorney, with 500 cases against collection agencies, referred to methods some use in the industry as "Tony Soprano tactics," referring to the mob boss in a popular television series. He said that "these mafia-like [illegal] tactics result in so much money" for the collection industry.[120] The Federal Trade Commission receives about 70,000 complaints about the industry each year.[121] Few investigations will be opened due to the lack of resources.

Approximately half (104) collection agencies in the Buffalo area received a failing grade from the Better Business Bureau due to unscrupulous tactics. Nationwide, 1 in 10 complaints about collection tactics originated in Western New York.[122] There has been no public concern expressed from faith communities anywhere in New York. At the same time the economy is employing thousands of persons in the collection

---

[119] "Dad Says Debt Collector Harassed 10-Year-Old," WFTV.com, June 30, 2010."

[120] Phillips, "Woman Sues Debt Collector Over Husband's Death," CNN.com.

[121] Gomstyn, "Did Debt Collection Calls Kill this Man?"

[122] Carolyn Thompson and David B. Caruso, "Buffalo's Debt Collectors Accused of Bullying," Associated Press, January 5, 2010.

industry, it is also causing negative health, physical and spiritual, consequences.

In New York, courts are increasingly, but glacially skeptical of the claims by lawyers representing debt collectors. Consumer groups have long argued that courts in general behave as an extension of debt collectors. Courts often rely on their undocumented, unsubstantiated claims.[123]

In a 2009 law suit filed by the New York Attorney General, 101,000 court orders were alleged to have been wrongly issued to collect $5,474 per consumer. Legal notice was not provided to these individuals. The Attorney General charged that the legal process company retained by law firms and collection agencies "repeatedly and persistently falsified" legal documents.[124]

According to one Nassau County District Court Judge, a debt collection law firm didn't offer "a scintilla of evidence" in one case. Judge Michael A. Ciaffa said that "mistakes, errors, misdeeds and improper litigation practices" were widespread with "demonstrably false" assertions. In this particular case the law firm, Eltman, Eltman & Cooper, had been cited for violating ethical rules 18 times. It paid a mere $14,800 in penalties.[125]

---

[123] See in general William Glaberson, "In New York, Some Judges Are Now Skeptical About Debt Collectors' Claims," NYTimes.com, May 7, 2010.

[124] Jonathan D. Glater, "N.Y. Claims Collectors of Debt Used Fraud," NYTimes.com, July 23, 2009.

[125] Ibid.

"High volume debt collection law practices," wrote Judge Ciaffa in his opinion, "are subject to the same ethical rules as apply to lawyers handling any other civil litigation matter. While mistakes can be made by any law office, lawyers engaged in the collection of assigned debts seem especially prone to pursuing claims improperly, often at the expense of the most vulnerable members of our society."[126]

In April 2010, Judge Ciaffa refused to grant Citibank a judgment for unpaid balances with an annual rate of 29.990%. The judge found that its law firm, Cohen & Slamowitz, failed to establish Citibank as a national bank that would have enabled it to be exempt from the state's usury laws.[127]

In another case, Judge Philip S. Straniere in Staten Island likened the situation of a credit card company to the "Land of Oz, run by a Wizard who no one has ever seen." He added that the "Land of Credit Cards permits consumers to be bound by agreements they never sign, agreements they may never have received, subject to change without notice and the laws of a state other than those existing where they reside."[128]

---

[126] *Erin Services. Co., LLC v. Bohnet* 2010 NY Slip Op 50327 (U), 26 Misc 3d 1230 (A).

[127] *Citibank SD v. Jared K. Hansen* (No. 19450/09) District Court, Nassau County, April 23, 2010.

[128] Glater, "N.Y. Claims Collectors of Debt Used Fraud," NYTimes.com.

A December 2009 study by the District Council 37 New York City Municipal Employees Legal Services found that "of the 238 cases in which our office sought substantiation of the debt . . . 94.5% of the cases, the plaintiff failed to substantiate the debt. Even when the debt buyer did respond, rather than showing that the debt was owed, its own documentation often proved the opposite." The report further documented that "the cases in the study bear a common thread: in many instances debt buyers sued consumers when they clearly had no legitimate claims."[129]

The New York City Bar Association's Committees on New York Civil Court and Consumer Affairs released an April 2010 report finding that "There is a crisis in the process service industry in New York City. In 2009, 66% of the 241,195 consumer debt cases initiated resulted in default judgments, often after 'sewer service.'" Sewer services are defined as not notifying individuals that they are being sued. It "is so improper that the process server may just as well have thrown the papers down the sewer." The Bar Association calls process service in New York a "debacle."[130]

---

[129] Robert Martin (principal author) with Shelby Russ and Faye Robins, "Where's the Proof?" District Council 37 Municipal Employees Legal Services, December 2009.

[130] New York City Bar Association. "Out of Service – A Call to Fix the Broken Process Service Industry," April 2010.

A larger question is why debt collection attorneys who knowingly pursue such unscrupulous practices are not identified, reported, and disbarred? The legal profession polices itself. Clearly, it has not done an adequate job in the area of collection attorneys. Continued failure to disbar such lawyers in New York and other states may necessitate that the public demand state legislatures to provide greater oversight.

In Minnesota debtors are being arrested and jailed. Based on the statistics cited above the question arises whether it should ever happen. If not, then there are Minnesota lawyers, similar to those in New York that should be disbarred.[131] *The Minneapolis Star-Tribune* did investigative reporting highlighting the arrest of Minnesotans for not showing up to court. Collection companies buy charged-off debt and allegedly make efforts to contact the debtor. If he or she does not show up in court then the owner of the debt gets the court to issue an arrest warrant.[132] Between 2006-10 arrests for debt increased 60 % in Minnesota.[133] Arrests for debt also have been reported in Wisconsin, New Jersey, Arkansas, and Washington.[134]

---

[131] There are heroes among Minnesotan lawyers. Todd Murray is one of them. He is crusading against the injustice of credit card and collection agency exploitation. Chris Serres, "Death Won't Stop these Debt Collectors," StarTribune.com, September 22, 2010. Contact Todd at ToddMurrayLaw.com.

[132] Renee Martin, "In Minnesota, Debtors' Prison is Not a Thing of the Past," GlobalComment.com, June 24, 2010.

[133] Martha C. White, "America's New Debtor Prison: Jail Time Being Given to those Who Owe," WalletPop.com, July 15, 2010.

## *Personal and Corporate Responsibility*

Many believe that those who get into credit card debt should pay it off. Few would disagree. But personal responsibility should be balanced with corporate responsibility. Responsibility should include why rates can be set at any amount. Responsibility should include why companies issue credit cards to the working poor and struggling middle class who will have an extraordinarily difficult time paying off a card balance at a high interest rate. These business models have more to do with Darwinian capitalism than an equitable economic system. Responsibility should include good corporate citizenship.

In addition, it's far too simplistic and dismissive to place all the blame on card holders who allegedly had the "choice" or are personally responsible for accepting a credit card offer. It's incorrect to believe that consumer debt is caused simply by free choice. If such thinking prevailed then price gauging after a natural disaster need not be made illegal.

Divorce, unemployment, health problems, family emergencies, and death of a loved one are not choices. Yet they make up the primary reasons people seek bankruptcy. These circumstances are often unwanted realities of life. They can be

---

[134] Ibid. See also Joan Firstenberg, "Debtor's Prisons Making a Comeback for those with Unpaid Bills," DigitalJournal.com, July 20, 2010.

anticipated, but few prepare or are ready for them should they occur. No one plans on getting a divorce. No one plans that a loved one will die prematurely. No one plans that Wall Street bankers will engage in such unbridled greed and capitalist shenanigans that it will ripple through the economy causing unemployment. No one plans for a child or spouse to have major health care issues that drain savings and then maxes out credit cards. No one plans for disasters like Katrina and the BP oil spill that destroy homes and businesses.

No one chooses to have a Fair Isaac Credit (FICO) score based on the company's "analytics" assigned to them that can indefinitely impact every aspect of their financial life. No one chooses to be without recourse to challenge FICO or its self-described analytics that is a mystery to average Americans. Why is this New York Stock Exchange corporation allowed to financially control the lives of Americans with so little accountability?

There is also the flip side to the personal responsibility of using a credit card. There is the corporate responsibility by bankers not to exploit the working poor and middle class with credit card fees and interest rates that will make them a permanent revenue source. There is the responsibility by credit card companies not to develop business models with the intent to make individuals max out their credit cards.

There is the choice for collection agencies to treat all persons with respect, dignity, and humanity. There is the choice in choosing a fair profit over greed and unjust gain. There is the choice by credit score bureaus to demand far more documentation, though not yet legally required, from credit card and collection agencies. There is the personal responsibility by self-described Christians employed as executives in the financial services industries to set policies that are just and equitable reflecting corporate responsibility.

# Eucharist

The examples cited above are some of the reasons why Christian leaders need to broaden their discussions about economic justice and establish some type of ethical standard for short-term consumer loans. "Every economic decision and institution," according to the U.S. Catholic Bishop's Conference, "must be judged in light of whether it protects or undermines the dignity of the human person."[135]

Although there are several potential models to further explore the issue, the journey toward God is both an individual and communal one which makes an analysis within a mystical Eucharistic approach worth pursuing.

The Mystical Supper, "the fount and apex of the whole Christian life,"[136] is the celebration of the new covenant. It is the living embodiment of the Sermon on the Mount. The Eucharist goes beyond a memorial for Jesus or his ministry. It is the challenge to live the Gospel with meaning and passion. Otherwise, it would be nothing more than an empty, fanciful ancient ritual. It is spiritual liberation and empowerment.

---

[135] U.S. Catholic Bishops. *Pastoral Letter on Catholic Social Teaching and the U.S. Economy.* Office for Social Justice. 1986.

[136] Walter M. Abbott, ed., The Documents of Vatican II (New York: Guild Press, 1966), 28.

John Paul II reflected that "Christians who gather each Sunday to experience and proclaim the presence of the Risen Lord are called to evangelize and bear witness in their daily lives." They are asked to make their whole life "a spiritual sacrifice pleasing to God."[137] The Eucharist is a never-ending call to take action for Jesus.

St. John Chrysostom taught that by taking Eucharist "We become one body; members, as it is said, of His flesh and of His bones ... His has mingled His body with ours that we may be one ..."[138] As Uncreated Light's children and disciples of Jesus who have been mystically united with Christ what should our individual and collective ministry be toward those who are denied housing or student loans due to a credit score?

Shared Eucharist means we participate in one another's joys, pains, and sufferings. Apostle Paul warned that whomever "eats this bread or drinks this cup of the Lord in an unworthy manner will be guilty of the body and blood of the Lord" (1 Corinthians 11:27). Paul is disturbed by excess food and wine that makes what should be a sacred gathering into a gluttonous feast. In a modern context it speaks to an excess of profit through high interest rates. Unjust gain causes the marginalization of personhood. It causes indifference.

---

[137] John Paul II, *Go in Peace* (Chicago: Loyola Press, 2003), 131-132.

[138] Vladimir Lossky, *The Mystical Theology of the Eastern Church* (Crestwood: St. Vladimir's Seminary Press, 1998), 180.

Christ reminds Christians through the Eucharist that each child of the Unchanging Spirit is loved completely. Despite religion's unfortunate contributions to capitalist sacralization and commoditization, the Mystical Supper has room for only love. Wealth, titles, degrees, or the emptiness of consumerism cannot eclipse or overpower the Holy Supper. The Holy Meal is the great equalizer where one child of the Divine Parent is no better than another. It is equality before God.

At the end of the Mass or Divine Liturgy Christians are told to "go in peace" back into the world. What is expected having returned to the secular community? Christians must bring back part of the kingdom in word and deed. St. John Damascene taught that we are "united also with all those who partake with us."[139] This means beyond those who attend a Mystical Supper with us in-person. It includes everyone, everywhere who have come together to accept the gift of life. There is a duty to those who suffer in another city, state, or country as well as members of the parish family.

Philosopher Boris Vysheslavtsev wrote that the ethical doctrine of Christ could be "expressed in a single symbol, the 'kingdom of God.' This is his 'revelation,' his 'good news,' and his 'New Testament.'" "It is the ultimate goal of human

---

[139] Lossky, *The Mystical Theology of the Eastern Church*, 181.

strivings."[140] It is the Eucharist that brings the individual to this goal through the family of Christ.

The Sacrifice is the spiritual conscience to religion when it is not stopping injustice or identifying and addressing basic needs of the Holy Author's people. Today, this spiritual conscience is calling Christian leaders to step back and reassess their respective ministries whether it's the prosperity gospel, religious groups accepting donations through credit cards, or allowing faith to be Americanized and hence secularized by making sacrosanct an economy in need of change.

## *Justice*

The Eucharist transforms justice from a secular "procedural matter"[141] to Christological activism – the kingdom of Enfolding Mystery at work in daily life. Eucharist justice never fails. It can never be bought, especially at the expense of someone's personhood or spiritual integrity.

It is the holiness that transcends the secular, temporal obligations to civil laws that can be unjust that good citizens are

---

[140] B.P. Vysheslavtsev, *The Eternal in Russian Philosophy* (Grand Rapids: William B. Eerdmans Publishing Company, 2002), 30.

[141] Gurian, Incarnate Love – Essays in Orthodox Ethics (Notre Dame: Indiana, 2002), 160-161.

expected to obey like the unregulated use of credit scores or high credit card interest rates. It is comparable to Aristotle's understanding that a person can act unjustly and still meet his or her obligations under secular law. [142]

If Christians are genuine followers of Jesus and faithful to the mission of the Eucharist then they cannot compartmentalize by rationalizing duty to unjust secular law. This is not a call for civil disobedience, though as Dr. Martin Luther King Jr. showed it does have its place. Instead, this is a call to publicly speak out against a system with significant, negative consequences for individuals and families. It's a call to put a human face on the "debtor," "credit card user," and "consumer with a poor credit score." There is a long overdue need to humanize those abused by the current economic structure.

"What we owe to each other," wrote economist Amartya Sen, "is an important subject for intelligent reflection."[143] Sen's focus is less on "terms of institutions, but rather in terms of the lives and freedoms of the people involved."[144] This dramatically shifts the discussion away from

---

[142] Ibid., 94.

[143] Amartya Sen, *The Idea of Justice*, (Cambridge: Belknap Press of Harvard University Press, 2009), 32-33.

[144] Ibid., xii. Sen observes that in "confining attention almost exclusively to Western literature, the contemporary – and largely Western – pursuit of

institutions that in theory are meant to create an ideal or just society to corrective or remedial justice as applied to individuals in their everyday lives.

Although Sen's approach is secular, it does have a Tolstoy-humanism to it that is relational, communal, and values human dignity. It is a fuller, richer understanding of Aristotle's justice. Service to the kingdom of God is "to contribute to the establishment of the greatest possible union between all living beings ..."[145] In the context of credit card issues, it is seeing faces, understanding lives, and feeling the pain that millions suffer. Our sisters and brothers are not statistics. They are persons who are hurting on multiple levels.

The *Philokalia* teaches that if the Maker of All Good is "praised through justice" then it "establishes the just mean in every undertaking, so that there will be no falling short ..."[146] Justice is the relationship between Creator and the Created. Duncan B. Forrester addressed scriptural justice as "something we hope for" and "setting matters right so that people can live together in peace."[147]

---

political philosophy in general and of the demands of justice in particular has been, I would argue, limited and to some extent parochial," xiv.

[145] Leo Tolstoy, *The Kingdom of God is Within You* (Mineola, New York: Dover Publications, Inc., 2006), 325.

[146] St. Nikodimos and St. Makarios, *The Philokalia – the Complete Text Vol. III* (London: Faber and Faber, 1995), 258.

[147] Gill. *The Cambridge Companion to Christian Ethics*, 198.

The Christian response to the spiritual, emotional, and physical consequences of debt, regardless of whether it is brought on by free choice, should be love and compassion. Eucharist justice is a spiritual and emotional response to the pain that a family or individual experiences due to hardship that can lead to despair, loneliness, isolation, hopelessness, and an array of health problems. An act of love brings healing, fellowship, and wholeness through the Eucharist. Christians must "dwell together in unity" (Psalm 133:1). It is a demonstrative act of being my brother and sister's keeper.

Injustice can be defined by the consequences caused by consumer debt – high interest rates, tactics by collection agencies, and the impact a negative credit score can have on housing, education[148], employment, or a person's physical and emotional wellbeing. Even if it were to be conceded for discussion purposes that the person chose to go into debt, no one chose to be spending a large percentage of their disposable income servicing debt. Nor does someone choose to forego peace of mind when the unintended consequences of collection calls begin.

---

[148] See Alex Ginsberg, "Debt Collector's ID Snafu 'Ruins My Life'," NYPost.com, September 8, 2009. An inaccurate credit score caused college loans of a young woman to be cancelled forcing her to both drop out of college and forego medical school.

In the recession starting at the end of 2008 and still continuing in 2010, 6.4 million Americans have been unemployed for six months or more. According to one finance writer, "Such long-term unemployment can do serious damage to personal credit."[149]

In February 2010, there were over 15 million unemployed Americans.[150] In October, the Bureau of Labor Statistics reported a September unemployment rate of 9.6%. "Underemployment," defined as persons working less than full-time unable to find proper or good-paying jobs, rose to 17.1%.[151]

Orthodox priest and theologian Sergius Bulgakov referred to men and women as the "economic logos of the world." Work is to produce. It is to create. It is a connection to nature and the Creator. He believed it to be a kind of "economic ministry" with "religious responsibility."[152] Bulgakov understood it as the duty of the individual to work for him- or herself that provides for the necessities of life (2 Thessalonians

---

[149] John W. Schoen, "Bad Credit Sidelines some Jobless Workers," MSNBC.com, February 23, 2010.

[150] Peter S. Goodman, "Millions Face Years Without Jobs," MSNBC.com (*New York Times* reprint), February 21, 2010.

[151] John Keefe, "September Employment Report, with Jobless Rate at 9.6%, Confirms Slow Recovery," MoneyWatch.bnet.com, October 8, 2010.

[152] Sergius Bulgakov, *The Orthodox Church* (Crestwood: St. Vladimir's Seminary Press, 1988), 167.

3:10-12). Individuals with a work ethic are denied an opportunity not only to support themselves or a family, but to have the dignity that comes from gainful employment.

As noted earlier, ten to sixteen million Americans are "suffering terribly due to their debts"[153] causing a new medical condition called "Debt Stress Syndrome"[154] According to a May 2010 Associated Press-GfK poll, 46 percent of Americans surveyed described debt stress as a "great deal" or that they were stressed "quite a bit" from it.[155]

Christianity has always focused on the "dignity of the human person."[156] The quality of justice is determined, in part, by how the nation's economy aids or hinders personal dignity.[157] It is also determined by its willingness to identify societal wrongs and the commitment to confront and stop an injustice.

---

[153] "Poll: Stress of Debt Takes Physical Toll," CNN.com, June 8, 2008.

[154] "Coping with 'Debt Stress Syndrome'," CBSNews.com, June 8, 2008.

[155] Jeannine Aversa, "Poll Finds Debt-Dogged Americans Stressed Out," DailyFinance.com, May 30, 2010.

[156] Chuck Collins and Mary Wright. *The Moral Measure of the Economy* (Maryknoll, New York: Orbis Books, 2007), 18.

[157] U.S. Catholic Bishops. *Pastoral Letter on Catholic Social Teaching and the U.S. Economy.* Office for Social Justice. 1986.

## *My Sister and Brother's Keeper*

Christians are called to be good stewards of that which they've been given. It's something self-described Christians should keep in mind who work in the collection, credit card, and credit bureau industries. Related to this stewardship is how it impacts one's neighbor and the greater community.

The Holy Communal Meal is a clear directive against oppressing those who share in the same covenant with UnCreated Light (Amos 5:6-7). How can Christians be their sister or brother's keeper, to love them – if they are unwilling to share in the Holy Feast? The invitation requires interaction, to grieve for him or her when there is misfortune and to celebrate with the sister or brother when there is prosperity.[158]

In light of the harsh consequences that are and will continue to occur, can disinterested Christians say meaningfully that they love their neighbor? Although Christ's blood is love, hope, and redemption, among other things, it is also the holy drink of suffering (Mark 14:35-36). It calls our attention to the emotional and physical pain of those around us.

The Hebrew Scriptures and New Testament often remind the faithful that they are only caretakers. All the blessings from the earth and under the heavens are temporarily made available before leaving this world. "The earth is the

---

[158] Helen Bacovcin, trans., *The Way of a Pilgrim – and the Pilgrim Continues His Way* (New York: Image Books, 1992), 115.

Lord's, and all its fullness," according to Apostle Paul quoting Psalm 24:1(1 Corinthians 10:26). It is the Governor of the Universe who created and through grace empowers humankind to benefit and build upon the gifts provided (Genesis 1:1). This includes financial gain.

## *Forgiveness*

The Mystical Supper is a new beginning that empowers followers of Jesus to right the world's wrongs. According to the Episcopalian catechism, the Eucharist calls Christians to "be in love and charity with all people."[159] This can include the mistreatment of others due to financial burdens.

It parallels, if not fulfills, the Almighty's call in Hebrew Scriptures to forgive indebtedness and return land to the original owner. Although this can be called mercy or justice, it seems more appropriate to view it as glorifying the Creator since everything belongs to the Maker of All Good. It shows that the Covenant of the Lover of All has been kept (Deuteronomy 6:25).

---

[159] *Book of Common Prayer* (Seabury Press, 1979), 860.

The Book of Jubilees called for the return of land, freedom for slaves, and debt forgiveness in the forty-ninth[160] year which has similarities to Christ's call to forgive seven times seven (Leviticus 25:1-55; Matthew 18:21). It reminds us that keeping Unchanging Spirit's ordinances and judgments will permit the people to "dwell in the land in confidence" (Leviticus 25:18). Making bankruptcy more accessible along with scaling back credit card interest rates will bring about a much needed modern economic Jubilation.

Ultimately, families and individuals that provide financial institutions steady revenue through minimum card payments become the "personal servants" of banks instead of the Creator (Leviticus 25:39-55). Jubilation returns to God that which always belonged to the Creator. It corrects an imbalance. Christians should think about Jubilation in the context of consumer debt.

The Prophets were particularly concerned about financial exploitation. Amos, first of the Israelite prophets, warned Yahweh's people that one of their offenses involved debt. They "sold the righteous for silver and the poor for a pair of sandals. They trample the heads of the poor into the dust of the earth" (Amos 2:6-7). Amos is likely to have been referring to situations where children were sold into slavery to pay debts (2 Kings 4:1-7) and the taking of clothes as pledge from the poor to

---

[160] Joseph b. Lumpkin, trans. *The Book of Jubilees* (Blountsville, AL: Fifth Estate, 2006).

secure loans (Exodus 22:25; Deuteronomy 24:12-13, 17).[161] Justice is no more (Amos 6:12). Hubris has taken hold complemented by an attitude of entitlement by those in positions to end the injustice (Amos 5:14; 5:18-20).[162]

Isaiah carries a similar message warning of the greed that inflicts God's people. Woe to those "who join house to house, who add field to field, to take something from their neighbor" (Isaiah 5:8). Is there a just interest rate for the poor and middle class that is not unjust gain, but equitable to all parties? Those who have taken unjustly will be "fed as bulls" (Isaiah 5:17). Micah criticizes the religious leaders of his day for their greed (Micah 3:5-7). Many religious leaders today support the prosperity gospel. In other cases those who are complacent have enabled an air of legitimacy over current financial practices. Collective Christian leadership has been absent in agitating for reform.

St. Tikhon of Zadonsk reminded those charging interest that though a person "took a loan from you is truly your debtor" "you are God's debtor" too. "He is indebted to you for material things, but you are indebted to God for sins. His debt is very

---

[161] John W. Miller, Meet the Prophets (New York: Paulist Press, 1987), 54.

[162] See also Ibid., 58 & 63. Miller observes that there are "striking similarities" between the "unregulated economic conditions in Israel in Amos' time, and the gravitation of economic power into the hands of a few elite" to the economic inequities of today. "Modern history is rife with examples of how dreadfully easy it is to ignore the plight of the destitute, if you are wealthy," according to Miller. "Tragically, only too often religion continues to buffer and protect rather than challenge the decadent lifestyles of these privileged elites."

small against your debt of sin, it is as though it were nothing." He advised, "Spare the poor that God may spare you."[163]

It's not just the debt that can't be paid that merits some level of forgiveness, but also the spiritual forgiveness of those policy makers, many of whom Christians, who have put in place or protected a system that entraps so many people. It is a call to love, bless, and pray for those who have contributed to the financial burden (Matthew 5:43-46).

In applying a more standard definition of Christian forgiveness toward both the lender and the debtor blame becomes irrelevant. Rather than get into a debate about greed, excess profit, or a borrower's irresponsibility, equity and justice would be better served by looking at consequences and finding a just resolution.[164]

"We have all hurt God."[165] It's a profound, powerful observation to reflect on. How often does the average Christian

---

[163] St. Tikhon of Zadonsk, *Journey to Heaven* (Jordanville, NY: Holy Trinity Monastery, 1994) 133.

[164] See in general Everett L. Worthington Jr., *A Just Forgiveness – Responsible Healing without Excusing Injustice* (Downers Grove, IL: IVP Books, 1984). Worthington doesn't necessarily have something as mundane as forgiveness in the context outlined here, but rather things that by comparison are far more egregious like the Holocaust or individual physical assaults from domestic violence. Yet in the broadest sense "forgiveness" offers a level of positive perspective to address a problem as it exists rather than get into a needless distraction of blame. See also Robert L. Browning and Roy A. Reed, *Forgiveness, Reconciliation, and Moral Courage* (Grand Rapids: William B. Eerdmans Publishing Company, 2004).

[165] Ibid.

think in those terms? It's not mere disobedience, but "hurting" the Holy Parent. How does the person hurt God individually and collectively by failing to act on behalf of sisters and brothers in the Body of Christ? The absence of love, compassion, and empathy for neighbor (Leviticus 19:18).

As Christians approach the Eucharist they must prepare themselves. They must be spiritually cleansed. In the Episcopal tradition of the Penitential Order the priest and people come before a merciful God to "confess that we have sinned against you in thought, word, and deed, by what we have done, and by what we have left undone." It is an admission that the penitent has not loved the Creator with his or her whole heart and "have not loved our neighbors as ourselves." Forgiveness is sought before receiving Holy Communion so that the Christian can "delight in your will and walk in your ways."[166]

Although public confession is not practiced in the Eastern Church, the Divine Liturgy is filled with references of forgiveness. One of the most often used responses is "Lord, have mercy" referring to the unworthy sinner. The priest's silent prayer during the Liturgy includes asking the Lover of Mankind to "make us worthy with a pure conscience to partake of Thy heavenly and awe-inspiring Mysteries ... from this holy and spiritual table for the forgiveness of sins, for the pardon of offenses ..."[167]

---

[166] *The Book of Common Prayer*, Penitential Order II.

What are the responsibilities of Christians after they have received the benefit of God's forgiveness? Christians are called back into the world to act on their faith. Forgive those who hurt us, perhaps a creditor or collection agency, and find ways, like in the days of Jubilation, to forgive or at least ameliorate the financial burdens of sisters and brothers. It is a directive to make sacred relationships with one another in the family of God while de-sacralizing an economy needing reform.

## *Thirst for Righteousness*

Scripture determines normal Christian behavior, according to one Orthodox theologian. It defines the community of Christ.[168] According to two other theologians, ethics reflects a realization of God's Creation as intended. It measures humankind's journey toward Pure Light. It is the

---

[167] Both the Ukrainian Byzantine Catholic and Ukrainian Eastern Orthodox Divine Liturgy of Saint John Chrysostom use almost identical prayers. See *My Divine Friend* (Yorkton, Saskatchewan: The Redeemers voice, 1959) and *Prayer Book* (Winnipeg: Ecclesia Publishing Corporation of the Ukrainian Orthodox Church, 2000).

[168] Vigen Guroian, *Ethics After Christendom – Toward an ecclesial Christian Ethic* (Eugene, Oregon: Wipf & Stock Publishers, 1994), 79.

sojourn to find, observed another, the purpose of life.[169] It is the realization of love in humanity.[170]

Christians are called to be the salt of the earth and the light of the world because they are created in the Divine Image.[171] The faithful are called to the Eucharist "with proper dispositions" so that "their thoughts match their words" and they celebrate the Holy Sacrifice "knowingly, actively, and fruitfully."[172] Those who receive are deified.[173]

In deification Christians seek righteousness (Mathew 5:6). They must preserve Eternal Perfect's fulfilled covenant, influence the world by example as children of light (Mathew 5:13-14; John 12:36; 1 Thessalonians 5:5).

Even if the plight of debtors is in part by their own making it still doesn't excuse "luring consumers into debt waters," as Consumer Reports noted, "well over their head …"

---

[169] Aristotle Papanikolaou and Elizabeth H. Prodromou, eds., *Thinking through Faith – New Perspectives from Orthodox Christian Scholars* (Crestwood: St. Vladimir's Seminary Press, 2008), 185-186.

[170] Ibid., 24-24.

[171] Stanley Harakas, *Toward Transfigured Life – the Theoria of Eastern Orthodox Ethics (Brookline: Holy Cross Greek Orthodox School of Theology, 1983)*, 21 & 27.

[172] *The Documents of Vatican II*, 143.

[173] Daniel B. Clendenin, ed. *Eastern Orthodox Theology* (Grand Rapids: Baker Books, 2002), 26.

Creditors can't blame the class they created "then punish" them with "significantly higher interest rates and fees."[174]

Here are further reasons why Christians should call for Jubilation and better monitoring and regulation of unjust gain[175]:

- As of 2008, 78% America's households had one or more credit cards;
- As of June 2009, Visa credit had 309 million cards in circulation;
- As of September 2009, MasterCard had 211 million cards in circulation;
- In 2008, 26.5 billion credit card transactions occurred;
- About 88% of the credit card market were controlled by the top 10 card issuers in 2006;
- Almost 14% of disposable consumer income went to service debt in the 4th quarter of 2008;
- Almost 15% of U.S. families "had debt exceeding 40% of their income;"
- Young adult households spent about 24% of income on debt payments;

---

[174] David K. Shipler, *The Working Poor – Invisible in America* (New York: Alfred A. Knopf, 2004), 24.

[175] The statistic are paraphrased or taken directly from Ben Woolsey and Matt Schulz, "Credit Card Statistics, Industry Facts, Debt Statistics," CreditCards.com.

- As reported in April 2009, 34 million Americans have been late making a credit card payment and 18 million citizens have missed a payment;
- Based on an April 2009, 58 million Americans admit not paying bills in a timely manner;
- In 2009, $20.5 billion in penalty fees on credit cards will be assessed;
- According to a November 2007 survey, 90% of African-American families with an income between $10,000 and $24,999 had credit card debt;
- In April 2009, 9 in 10 undergraduates reported paying for direct education with credit cards; and
- Most people put credit card debt at the top of things not to be discussed.

Historically, Judeo-Christian values were not ambivalent about the charging of interest. Rabbis of ancient Israel condemned those who charged interest on money to fellow Jews. A usurer "denies the God of Israel." He commits an abomination comparable to the "shedders of blood." "Blessed is the one" who loans without usury.[176]

Basil of Caesarea (330-379), Gregory of Nyssa (330-395), and Gregory of Nazianzus (329-389) were among the early

---

[176] Abraham Cohen, "Everyman's Talmud – The Major Teachings of the Rabbinic Sages" (New York: Schocken, 1995), 195-196.

church leaders to speak against usury, defined more simply as the charging of interest.[177] Concern over unjust lending has continued to this day, but absent the passion and multiple voices that once existed.[178]

In July 2009, Pope Benedict XVI issued the encyclical *Caritas in Veritate* (Charity in Truth). In it the Bishop of Rome warned against profit becoming an exclusive goal. He noted that "if it is produced by improper means and without the common good as its ultimate end, it risks destroying wealth and creating poverty."[179] As noted earlier, Prof Elizabeth Warren has said that billions of dollars are taken from families due to credit card gimmicks.

The Pope further noted that the "dignity of the individual and the demands of justice require that economic choices do not cause disparities in wealth to increase in an excessive and morally unacceptable manner ... Justice must be applied to every phase of economic activity ... every economic

---

[177] See in general, Susan R. Holman, *The Hungry Are Dying: Beggars and Bishops in Roman Cappadocia* (New York: Oxford University Press, 2001) and Robert P. Maloney, "the Teach of the Fathers on Usury: An Historical Study on the Development of Christian Thinking," *Vigiliae Christianae*, Vol. 27, No. 4 (December 1973), 241-265.

[178] See especially, "the Theological Economics of Medieval Usury Theory," in *Bonds of Imperfection: Christian Politics, Past, and Present* (Grand Rapids: Wm. B. Eerdmans Publishing Company, 2003) by Oliver O'Donovan and Joan Lockwood O'Donovan.

[179] Thomas J. Reese, S.J., "Pope Benedict on Economic Justice," WashingtonPost.com, July 7, 2009.

decision has a moral consequence."[180] In light of the burdens caused by the credit card and collection industries his warning underscores an existing reality.

Consistent with history Christians have always been aware of the dangers that stem from various forms of economic disparity. What has changed, however, is the narrowness as to what is pursued as important social justice issues. Housing, education, and employment, for example, remain a top priority. Consumer debt must now be included.

The amount of money being used to service debt, not pay it off, should be factored into the equation of social justice. Although it's been unconvincingly argued that better regulating interest rates will deprive the poor or lower middle class access to credit, it seems disingenuous when a constant revenue source is created through high interest. It seems not having a credit card places a poor or lower middle class family in a much better financial position in the long-term.

According to Prof. Ronald J. Mann of Columbia Law School, of the families with incomes below $23,000, 31% of these household have credit card debt. "Among those that carry credit card debt, half have debt equal to 10% of their income and a quarter have debt equal to 25% of their income (all before making mortgage payments, car payments, child support

---

[180] Ibid.

payments and the like)." He adds further that "we must acknowledge that credit card use among poor households has created a debt . . . that many households will bear for years, if not decades."[181]

Forgotten again is the directive to "open [our] hands to [our] brother, to [our] poor and needy in [our] land" (Deuteronomy 15:1-11). Is indifference to the plight of the financially burdened cited above reflective of a hardened heart, a shut hand for the sister and brother, and the forgotten year of remission (Deuteronomy 15:7, 9)? Although it is troubling that the poor are burdened in this way, the focus should not be lost on the millions of Americans who are considered middle class that also struggle with debt issues.

Credit card companies, by the way, refer to those who pay off debt each month as "deadbeats" and "freeloaders." As noted earlier profit models are now based on the expectation that consumers don't pay off debt each month.[182]

---

[181] Ronald J. Mann, "Patterns of Credit Card Use Among Low and Moderate Income Households," Columbia.edu.

[182] Mike Konczal, "Should You Trust Visa to Teach You About Credit Cards?" TheAtlantic.com, November 17, 2009.

## *The Lord's Prayer*

In praying the Lord's Prayer, all Christians, offer ourselves" as "fellow workers" of the early disciples "for the Kingdom." The prayer demands "an unconditional and filial devotion to the interests of God."[183] Specifically in the Lord's Prayer all can hear the call to take action. The central Christian prayer, "show men how to love this Present God ... who induces in us a thirst and a longing that cannot be satisfied by any other thing than Himself alone."[184]

Although there is a general call to "re-conversion" in the Eucharist, it holds equally true to components of the Lord's Prayer. Re-conversion here is meant as a spiritual challenge. It is a conscious decision to ask whether the process of faith has become routine worship absent reflection. All Christians, for example, know the Lord's Prayer, but what does it mean and how is it applied in our daily life?

Speaking of prayer in general terms, St. Dimitri of Rostov said that to "pray means to stand before God with the mind ..." to gaze at the Creator, and to "converse" "in reverent fear and hope." St. Theophan more specifically said that prayer is "standing with the mind in the heart before God" that

---

[183] Evelyn Underhill, *Abba – Meditations Based on the Lord's Prayer* (New York: Vintage Books, 2003), 147.

[184] Ibid., 152.

includes the Creator's glorification.[185]   Ss. Nikodimos and Makarios referred to prayer as "a stimulus towards the divine."[186] In the Lord's Prayer the Christian finds among other things healing, forgiveness, repentance, and accountability to God.

Prof. Sider of the Sider Center on Ministry and Public Policy at Eastern Baptist Theological Seminary, has called for "practical ways to strengthen accountability in the Body of Christ."[187]   Although his focus is on church communities holding one another accountable through a kind of objective critique, his observation of "accountability in the Body of Christ" has a useful application to the entire Christian community of every denomination. The "practical application" of the Lord's Prayer may be one starting point.

Humankind's place in the universe is clear from the opening of the prayer. The Holy Author is in heaven. All Christians have in them "the spark of absolute life" in equal measure, no one better than the other.[188] It should draw attention to disparity among us and how it's caused.

---

[185] Igumen Chariton of Valamo, compiler. *The Art of Prayer – An Orthodox Anthology* (London: Faber and Faber, 1973), 16-17.

[186] St. Nikodimos of the Holy Mountain and St. Makarios of Corinth, *The Philokalia Vol. 2* (London: Faber and Faber, 1981), 25-26.

[187] Sider, *The Scandal of the Evangelical Conscience*, 110-114.

[188] Underhill, *Abba – Meditations Based on the Lord's Prayer,* 142.

God's name is hallowed. To show love, respect, and reverence cannot be achieved by a mere recitation of the prayer. Uncreated Light's holiness is shown by demonstrative acts in the world as we find it. Christians show God's hallowedness by letting the Creator work through them to serve a purpose greater than their own self-interest that includes social and economic justice.

Although the kingdom comes, it is also within every Christian heart (Luke 17:20-21). Christians are called and empowered to love unconditionally, without judgment. A manifestation of it would be to show compassion for the current plight of millions of Americans in debt. The kingdom within is also an active lay ministry to address the imbalance now in place so it does not continue to happen to others.

"Thy will be done," could be an approach for "God-given responsibilities" to the Creator and one another.[189] Yes, there is a responsibility to fulfill a promise to pay back a loan. There is also a Christian requirement to treat others fairly and equitably whether it involves a reasonable interest rate or identifying Christians working in the collection and credit card industries that have not fulfilled their responsibilities to the Giver of Life. Those in the industry are at the greatest spiritual risk, more so than those burdened by the harshness of seemingly

---

[189] Marshall, *Toward An Evangelical Public Policy*, .322.

endless debt cycle. To fulfill God's will is to love the neighbor who hurts as well as the neighbor who has gone spiritually astray and needs to be refocused.

The prayer is a humbling reminder that our daily bread is by and through the grace of God. By extension no one should take more than is needed. In doing so, deprivation of another sister or brother can occur.

Because we hurt the Lover of All by the mistreatment of others we do need ongoing forgiveness. Forgiveness, however, must be accompanied by reconciliation or a sincere effort to make things right. The Creator must be asked to teach us to be true to Creation as God intended. In short, how do we love?[190] How do we show it? Forcefully speaking out against unjust credit card interest rates, the tactics of collection agencies, and the harm a low credit score can cause is an expression of love?

---

[190] Alexander Men, *Son of Man* (Torrance: Oakwood Publications, 1998), 61.

*Full Circle*

The Mystical Supper demands the humility to acknowledge responsibility whether religion's improper role in making sacred an economic or political system; the family or individual's decision to use short-term borrowing on non-essentials that causes needless, ongoing debt; Christians within an industry that create marketing incentives for consumers to max out credit cards, set collection policies, fix high interest rates; or Christian members of Congress with power to better regulate the credit card, credit bureau, and collection agency industries.

The Eucharist is a sacrament. All sacraments, especially the Eucharist, occur through Holy Sophia. [191] The Eucharist is

---

[191] Sergei Bulgakov, *Sophia – the Wisdom of God* (Hudson, NY: Lindisfarne, Press, 1993), 138.

Christian identification of Wisdom specifically with the Holy Spirit, though not widespread, dates to at least Theophilus of Antioch (d.183?) and Irenaeus of Lyons (125?-202?). See William G. Rusch, *The Trinitarian Controversy – Sources of Early Christian Thought* (Philadelphia: Fortress Press, 1980), pp. 1-7. Theophilus discusses the role of Wisdom in *Apologia Ad Autolychum* (Advent.org and EarlyChristianWritings.com). See "Theophilus of Antioch and the 'Two Hands of God'," Theandros.com (Online Journal of Orthodox Christian Theology and Philosophy), Volume 4, Number 2, Winter 2006/2007. Irenaeus interchanges Wisdom of the Hebrew Scriptures with the Holy Spirit. He writes in *Against Heresies* of the "Spirit of wisdom and understanding, the Spirit of counsel and strength, the Spirit of knowledge and the fear of God came down upon the Lord . . . [God] entrusted [Jesus] to the Holy Spirit." (Vatican.va – prepared by the Spiritual Theology Department of the Pontifical University of the Holy Cross).

the starting point, the journey, the full, unbreakable spiritual circle of Christ. The Last Supper invites us to unite with the will of the Almighty. Two wills united as one "so that together with God we can do good and creative things."[192] This includes reaffirming the "royal dignity" of man and woman created in the image of the Creator.[193]

---

Modern Sophiology traces its roots to the eighteenth century. Ukrainian philosopher Hryhorij Savyc Skovoroda (1722-1794) may have been one of the first modern advocates within Eastern Orthodoxy of the world's "feminine essence." See Richard H. Marshall, Jr. and Thomas E. Bird, eds., *Hryhorij Savyc Skovoroda – An Anthology of Critical Articles* (Edmonton: Canadian Institute of Ukrainian Studies Press, 1994), 209.

There is a maternal element here that all too often gets confused with Our Blessed Lady. Nature, which Sophia can be associated with in light of her role as "craftsman" at the time of Creation, can be as awe-inspiring as she can be frightening. She can be as calm and still as she can be earth-shaking. She can destroy through fire and use fire to create new life. In the very beginning, starting in the second verse of the first book, Sophia is mentioned at the time of creation. "The Spirit of God" hovered over "the face of the water" (Genesis 1:2). Scholars and theologians have widely understood this to be the Holy Spirit. See in general the annotations in the *Orthodox Study Bible* (New King James Version), (Nashville: Thomas Nelson, 2008) edited and annotated by His Beatitude Metropolitan MAXIMOS, Michel Najim, and Joseph Allen. *The New Oxford Annotated Bible* (Oxford: Oxford University Press, 2007) notes in a footnote that interpreters "have tended to see the 'Spirit' of the Trinity," but that "wind" "fits the ancient context better," p. 11.

[192] Mary B. Cunningham and Elizabeth Theokritoff, *The Cambridge to Orthodox Christian Theology* (Cambridge: University Press, 2008), 82.

[193] Ibid., 84.

# Living the Faith

Eucharist is Jesus Alive. The Holy Meal is the Liturgy on fire. Jesus is not asking to be memorialized. He is not dead. Celebrating the Last Supper is transforming the world with spiritual sustenance (Mark 14:22-26; Matthew 26:26-29; and Luke 22:14-23).

It confronts harm, suffering, or another form of injustice. Every follower of Jesus must take up the cross to continue Christ's work in a different cultural setting. If the Eucharist "is to be sincere and thorough, it must lead to various works of charity and mutual help … and to different forms of Christian witness."[194] The Holy Supper shows that "human life is integrated in Christ's personal life" and "all human sufferings are contained" in the sufferings of Jesus.[195]

Metropolitan Andrey Sheptytsky, a revered Eastern Rite Catholic prelate, said that Christ sought an equal distribution of wealth. It is "the best foundation for the economic strength of a people, because it is strength founded not on an overall

---

[194] *The Documents of Vatican II*, 545-546.

[195] Sergius Bulgakov, *The Holy Grail & the Eucharist* (Hudson, NY: Lindisfarne Books, 1997), 53.

accumulation of goods, but rather on a median wealth for all of its citizens."[196]

In context to this discussion it is a call to elevate borrowers to a fairer contractual or commercial position with the lending counterpart. It requires greater equity that neutralizes an extreme commercial advantage at the expense of the borrower. This does not suggest a lender should forgo a fair profit. It's a call to bring equilibrium to the relationships that are lacking it. Profit or wealth in itself is not bad. The means or process to obtain it, however, can become destructive on several different levels.

Legal consideration should be given to defining usury as an excessive rate of interest that has the potential to be destructive to the family or individual. Calling usury something beyond a statutorily allowable rate is inadequate.

Linking interest charged by the Federal Reserve for loaning money to banks should be explored in connection with consumer credit. Banks often benefit from lower Federal Reserve rates, but this may have little impact on short-term consumer borrowing.[197]

---

[196] Peter Galadza, *The Theology and Liturgical Work of Andrei Sheptytsky (1865-1944)* (Ottawa: Metropolitan Andrey Sheptytsky Institute of Eastern Christian Studies at Saint Paul University, 2004), 186.

[197] In 2002, Tamara Draut wrote in the *Northwest Arkansas Times* that "over the last year and a half, Federal Reserve rate cuts have dramatically lowered interest rates on consumer loans, setting off a stampede of home refinancing, as well as new home and auto purchases. But such Fed inspired rate relief is

There are many other specific public policy proposals that can be made at the national level. They range from federal licensing of credit bureaus and collection agencies to prohibiting in most cases the use of credit scores for housing, employment, and education loans. Negative information should be removed as soon as a settlement has been reached or after five years. France has adopted a model worth considering.[198]

Federal standards and better oversight are necessary in calculating credit scores, how they're permitted to be used and by whom. Any information reported to a credit bureau should only be accepted with sufficient documentation. As noted earlier, the only responsibility a bureau has is to accurately record the information provided by a creditor. Verification of the information's accuracy is not required.

Documentation should especially be required showing an unbroken chain of title when debt has been sold by an

---

not happening everywhere: credit card rates remain staggeringly high. It's almost inconceivable – yet true – that in 2001, the Federal Reserve cut interest rates 11 times, yet the average credit card rate dropped by less than 1 percentage point." Paul Peter Jesep, "Spiritual Leaders: Rise Up vs. Usury," SeacoastOnLine.com, June 22, 2003.

[198] According to Niall McKay, "there are no credit-reporting agencies in France. Instead, the Banque de France manages a list of those who default on their loans. Once the bill is paid, the name is removed from the list, and even if the bill is not paid, the debtors' names are removed after five years. Further, the list is industry-specific, so credit card companies only have access to names held in the banking and financial databases. This is in sharp contrast to the U.S., where both positive and negative data is collected, files are managed by private companies and available across industries, and defaulted payments stay on the report long after a bill is paid." See the Frontline series *Secret History of the Credit Card* at PBS.org, November 23, 2004.

originator to a collection agency who may also sell it. Included in the documentation should be how and when the debt originated, the authorization the collector has to pursue it, how much was paid for the debt, and proof that the statute of limitations has not tolled.

Debt settlement companies also need to be reigned in. According to one consumer advocate, there are 9 million people in debt settlement plans that "are going to be hung out to dry." The Federal Trade Commission (FTC) reported that maybe 30% of consumers will get a settlement. Although new regulations have been put in place more are needed.[199]

A national, uniformed statute of limitations of five years is long overdue for uncollected debt along with harsh penalties for "re-aging zombie debt" – debt that was never owed or no longer collectable due to bankruptcy or the tolling of the statute of limitations, but is reported as collectable. In addition, once debt is delinquent or charged-off interest and penalties must be capped.

In the case of New York, the report cited earlier by the District Council 37 of the New York City Municipal Employees Legal Services recommends that debt collectors be prohibited

---

[199] Charles Wallace, "Consumers Face Huge Losses with Debt Settlement Firms," DailyFinance.com, August 31, 2010. See also Charles Wallace, "Losses Mount as Debt Settlement Firms Face New Rules," DailyFinance.com, September 13, 2010 and Peter S. Goodman, "Peddling Relief, Industry Puts Debtors in a Deeper Hole," NYTimes.com, June 18, 2010.

from initiating a lawsuit "unless it is in possession of enough evidence, in a form admissible in court" to show validity of the claim. Laws are lacking in New York, and no doubt in most states, that require a plaintiff to "set forth evidence of its claims when it files the lawsuit."[200]

Congress needs to re-visit the bankruptcy law. As it now exists there is no allowances made for unemployment, medical emergencies, natural disasters like Katrina, the British Petroleum (BP) disaster off the Gulf Coast, or fires that destroy homes and businesses. A Jubilee movement for the relief of personal debt merits as much focus as Christians have given to global debt relief for impoverished nations.[201]

Regardless of the willingness of Congress to act, priests, rabbis, mullahs, pastors, and other religious leaders should seriously consider modifying any social justice ministry to include the violations of civil, human, and privacy rights stemming from credit cards, credit bureaus, and collection agencies. It would make an extraordinary social statement if faith communities only took donations in the form of cash, check, money order, and debit card. The last three options could also apply to the purchase of religious or spiritual items on websites.

---

[200] "Where's the Proof?" District Council 37 New York City Municipal Employees Legal Services, December 2009.

[201] Collins and Wright, *The Moral Measure of the Economy*, 118.

Unions also have the opportunity to play an important role. Pension and retirement funds invest billions of dollars in the stock market. These investments need not include banks that charge excessive interest rates or retain collection companies with unscrupulous practices. Socially responsible investing can include an evaluation of a company's role in creating or exacerbating consumer debt.[202]

Teaching and sacramental ministries are complements.[203] The "greatest failure of the present-day Church lies in its failure to exercise a teaching ministry, and where there is failure in teaching, there must also be devaluation of the sacraments." Ironically, that's as true today as it was when William Barclay made the observation in 1967.[204] Re-teaching Christian fundamentals may help to address consumerism and credit card debt.

In reflecting on this aspect of the economy Christians, regardless of denomination, may wish to consider several questions – "Am I worthy of the Holy Sacrifice made by Jesus

---

[202] Ibid., 127. In September 2010, religious leaders and the United Auto Workers (UAW) declared their intent to withdraw hundreds of millions of dollars from JP Morgan Chase due to the bank's refusal to place a two year moratorium on foreclosures in Michigan and improve working conditions in North Carolina. See "UAW and Religious Leaders Plan to Pull Millions of Dollars from JPMorgan Chase," WZYA.com, September 24, 2010.

[203] William Barclay, *The Lord's Supper* (London: SCM Press LTD., 1967), 11.

[204] Ibid., 11.

celebrated in the Mystical Supper?" Or "Do I pray and live the Lord's Prayer with a heart of passion in my daily life?"

Finally, "What would Jesus do, the Creator's only child who chased out the money changers from the temple, in response to unjust gain evidenced by collection bureaus and credit card companies?" "What would Jesus say to those working in these industries that identify themselves as one of his followers?" It's not likely he'd say "collect and exploit more." Nor is it likely Jesus would remain silent.

Are you a follower of Jesus? If you are what will you do to help end the suffering, exploitation, and unjust gain caused by credit bureaus, collection agencies, and credit card companies? What personal responsibility will you assume?

# Bibliography

Abbott, Walter M., ed. *The Documents of Vatican II*. New York: Guild Press, 1966.

Abernethy, Bob. "Prosperity Gospel." *Religion & Ethics* (August 17, 2007). http://www.PBS.org.

Ackerman, James M. "Interest Rates and the Law: A History of Usury." *Arizona State Law Journal* 61(1981).

"Americans Falling Behind on Credit Card Payments at Alarming Rate." (December 24, 2007). http://www.FoxNews.com.

Anderson, Gary A. *Sin – A History*. New Haven: Yale University Press, 2009.

Aristotle. *Nicomachean Ethics*. New York: Barnes & Noble, 2004.

_____. *Politics*. Charleston: BiblioBazaar, 2008.

St. Anthanasius Orthodox Academy. *Orthodox Study Bible (NKJV)*. Nashville: Thomas Nelson Publishers, 1993.

Arnoldy, Ben. "The Spread of the Credit Check as Civil Rights Issue – Minorities are Starting to Fight Employers Over he Use of Credit History In Hiring." *Christian Science Monitor* (January 18, 2007). http://www.CSMonitor.com.

Aversa, Jeannine. "Poll Finds Debt-Dogged Americans Stressed Out." (May 30, 2010). http://www.DailyFinance.com.

Avila, Sergio. "Can Your Credit Score Cost You a Job? 9OYS Investigates," (May 21, 2010). http://www.KGUN9.com.

Bacovcin, Helen, trans. *The Way of a Pilgrim – and the Pilgrim Continues His Way*. New York: Image Books, 1992.

"Bank Bailout Could End Poverty for 50 Years – Oxfam Tells G20," Press Release. (April 1, 2009). http://www.Oxfam.org.

"Bank Losses Lead to Drop in Credit Card Debt," (September 25, 2010). http://www.CNBC.com.

Barclay, William. *The Lord's Supper*. London: SCM Press LTD, 1967.

_____. *The Mind of Jesus*. New York: Harper-Collins, 1976.

Barlow, Tom. "The New Food Stamp User Might Look a Lot Like You." (June 9, 2010). http://www.WalletPop.com.

Belsie, Laurent. "Credit Scores Slide Downward." (July 27, 2010). http://CSMonitor.com.

"Benny Hinn Runs Lucrative Operation." (September 1, 2008). http://www. ReligionNewsBlog.com

Berr, Jonathan. "Kenneth Feinberg Tries to Shame Wall Street." (July 23, 2010). http://www.DailyFinance.com.

Berr, Jonathan. "Military Families Struggle with Mounting Debts." (May 30, 2010). http://www.DailyFinance.com.

Black, Henry Campbell. *Black's Law Dictionary – 6th Edition.* St. Paul: West Publishing, 1990.

*Book of Common Prayer.* The Seabury Press, 1979.

Bourke, Vernon J. *History of Ethics Vol. 1 – Graeco-Roman to Early Modern Ethics.* Mount Jackson, VA: Axios Press, 1968.

_____. *History of Ethics Vol. 2 – Modern and Contemporary Ethics.* Mount Jackson, VA: Axios Press, 1968.

Breck, John. *God with Us – Critical Issues in Christian Life and Faith.* Crestwood: St. Vladimir's Seminary Press, 1997.

_____. *Longing for God – Orthodox Reflections on Bible, Ethics, and Liturgy.* Crestwood: St. Vladimir's Seminary Press, 2006.

Brill, Steven. "Government for Sale: How Lobbyists Shaped the Financial Reform Bill." (July 1, 2010). http://www.Time.com.

Brown, Raymond E., Joseph A. Fitzmyer, and Roland E. Murphy, eds. *The Jerome Biblical Commentary.* Englewood Cliffs: Prentice-Hall, Inc., 1968.

Browning, Robert L. and Roy A. Reed. *Forgiveness, Reconciliation, and Moral Courage – Motives and Designs for Ministry in a Troubled World.* Grand Rapids: William B. Eerdmans Publishing Company, 2004.

Bulgakov, Sergius. *The Bride of the Lamb.* Grand Rapids: William B. Eerdmans Publishing Company, 20002.

_____. *The Holy Grail & the Eucharist*. Hudson, NY: Lindisfarne Books, 1997.

_____. *The Orthodox Church*. Crestwood: St. Vladimir's Seminary Press, 1988.

"Career Profiles Show Lawmakers' 16 Year Fundraising Totals," (March 8, 2005). http://www.OpenSecrets.org.

Catholic Biblical Association of America. *The New American Bible*. Huntington, Indiana: Our Sunday Visitor Inc., 1976.

Chariton of Valamo, Igumen. *The Art of Prayer – An Orthodox Anthology* London: Faber and Faber Limited, 1973.

Cheves, John. "Critics: Reform Backed by McConnell Fostered Crisis," (October 2, 2008). http://www.Kentucky.com.

Chu, Kathy and Sandra Block. "As Lenders Clamp Down, Credit Scores Take a Hit," (September 23, 2009). http://www.USAToday.com

*Citibank SD v. Hansen* (No. 19450/09 District Court, Nassau County, April 23, 2010).

Clapsis, Emmanuel. "Wealth and Poverty in Christian Tradition." *Holy Cross Greek Orthodox School of Theology – online library of the Church of Greece*. http://www.myriobiblos.gr. (accessed July 2009).

Clendenin, Daniel B., ed. *Eastern Orthodox Theology*. Grand Rapids: Baker Academic, 2003.

Cohen, Abraham. *Everyman's Talmud – The Major Teachings of the Rabbinic Sages*. New York: Schocken, 1995.

Collins, Church and Mary Wright. *The Moral Measure of the Economy*. Maryknoll, NY: Orbis Books, 2007.

Collins, Margaret. "Credit History for Insurance, Hiring Eyed by Congress," (May 12, 2010). http://www.BusinessWeek.com.

Connelly, Eileen JA. "Americans' Credit Scores at New Lows." (July 12, 2010). http://www.MSNBC.com.

Coogan, Michael D. *The New Oxford Annotated Bible*. Oxford: University Press, 2007.

Crane, Amy Buttell. "Bankruptcy Law Another Blow for Katrina Victims," (September 2005). http://www.BankRate.com.

"Credit Card Debt 'could be halved by interest rate cap'." (October 20, 2010). WHICH4U.co.uk.

Cunningham, Mary B. and Elizabeth Theokritoff. *The Cambridge Companion to Orthodox Christian Theology*. Cambridge: University Press, 2008.

Curran, Charles E. *American Catholic Social Ethics*. Notre Dame: University of Notre Dame Press, 1982.

"Dad Says Debt Collector Harassed 10-Year-Old." (June 30, 2010). WFTV.com.

Dante. *The Divine Comedy: Volume 1: Inferno*. New York: Penguin Classics, 2002.

Davis, William. "Average Credit Card Rates Higher than 14 Percent." (October 12, 2010). http://www.CreditNet.com.

Detweiler, Gerri. "Understanding the Credit Card Accountability Responsibility and Disclosure Act of 2009." http://www.Credit.com (accessed June 2009).

*The Divine Liturgy according to St. John Chrysostom.* Ontario: The Basilian Press, 1987.

*The Divine Liturgy according to St. John Chrysostom.* Minneapolis: Light and Life Publishing, 1989.

Dobson, Caroline. "Senate Wall Street Reforms Stall Credit Card Overhaul." (May 20, 2010). http://www.TheEpochTimes.com.

Elliot, Calvin. *Usury.* Charleston: Bibliobazaar, 2007.

Epstein, Jonathan D. "Hamburg Debt Collector is Slapped for $125,000." (July 28, 2010). http://www.BuffaloNews.com.

*Erin Services. Co., LLC v. Bohnet* 2010 NY Slip Op 50327 (U), 26 Misc 3d 1230 (A).

"Factbox – Some Financial Reforms Missing from US Legislation." (June 30, 2010). http://www.Reuters.com.

"Fact Sheet: Reforms to Protect American Credit Card Holders." Press Release (May 22, 2009). http://www.WhiteHouse.gov.

Feyerick, Deborah. "Ex-Bankers on Pushing Customers to Rack Up Debt." (September 25, 2008). http://www.CNN.com.

"FICO Scores Sink to a New Low for Americans: Morgan Drexen Asks Are FICO Scores Realistic?" (July 22, 2010). http://www.PRWeb.com

Firstenberg, Joan. "Debtor's Prisons Making a Comeback for those with Unpaid Bills." (July 20, 2010). http://www.DigitalJournal.com.

Fountain, Rev. Timothy. "My Voice: Loss of Credit Card Jobs Sign of Better Times." (September 17, 2010). http://www.ArgusLeader.com.

Frank, Robert H. "Income Inequality: Too Big to Ignore." (October 16, 2010). http://www.NYTimes.com.

Galadza, Peter. *The Theology and Liturgical Work of Andrei Sheptytsky (1865-1944)*. Ottawa: Metropolitan Andrey Sheptytsky Institute of Eastern Christian Studies, 2004.

Gill, Robin, ed. *The Cambridge Companion to Christian Ethics*. Cambridge: University Press, 2001.

Ginsberg, Alex. "Debt Collector's ID Snafu 'Ruins My Life'." *New York Post* (September 8, 2009). http://www.NYPost.com.

Glater, Jonathan D. "N.Y. Claims Collectors of Debt Used Fraud." *New York Times* (July 23, 2009). http://www.NYTimes.com.

Glover, Stephen. "Sorry, But I Agree with Most of What Mr Cable Says. Pity About the Posturing." (September 22, 2010). http://www.DailyMail.co.uk.

Gomstyn, Alice. "Did Debt Collection Calls Kill this Man?" (September 22, 2009). http://www.ABCNews.com.

Goodman, Peter S. "Millions Face Years without Jobs." (February 21, 2010). http://www.MSNBC.com.

_____. "Peddling Relief, Industry Puts Debtors in a Deeper Hole." (June 18, 2010). http://www.NYTimes.com.

Goodstein, Laurie. "Believers Invest in the Gospel of Getting Rich," *New York Times*. (August 16, 2009).

Graves, Steven M. and Christopher L. Peterson. "Usury Law and the Christian Right: Faith-Based Political Power and the Geography of American Payday." *Loan Regulation, 57 Catholic University Law Review* 637 (Spring 2008).

Gross, Karen. "Credit Card Companies Won't Quit." (March 21, 2010). http://www.TimesUnion.com.

Grube, George W. *The Complete Book of Orthodox*. Salisbury, MA: Regina Orthodox Press, 2001.

Guroian, Vigen. *Ethics After Christendom – Toward an Ecclesial Christian Ethic* Eugene, OR: Wipf & Stock Publishers, 1994.

_____. *Incarnate Love – Essays in Orthodox Ethics.* Notre Dame: University of Notre Dame Press, 2002.

Hadley, Michael L. ed. *The Spiritual Roots of Restorative Justice.* Albany: State University of New York Press, 2001.

Harakas, Stanley S. *Contemporary Moral Issues Facing the Orthodox Christian.* Minneapolis: Light and Life Publishing Company, 1982.

_____. *Toward Transfigured Life – the Theoria of Eastern Orthodox Ethics.* Brookline: Holy Cross Greek Orthodox School of Theology, 1983.

Harris, Dan and Andrew Sullivan. "Is the American Dream Dead – Or Just in Hiding?" (June 16, 2009). http://www.ABCNews.com.

Hawkins, Asher. "Credit Card Customers Punished for Doing the Right Thing?" ABCNews.com, April 11, 2010.

Holman, Susan R. *The Hungry Are Dying: Beggars and Bishops in Roman Cappadocia.* New York: Oxford University Press, 2001.

Hopson, Judi Light, Emma H. Hopson, and Ted Hagen, "Credit Card Debt Can Wreck Relationships," (May 17, 2010). http://www.SeattleTimes.com.

Housser, Andrew, "More Credit Card Rules Take Effect August 22nd with CARD Act," (August 9, 2010). http://www.WTEN.com.

"How to Keep Tabs on Your Credit Report." (April 29, 2010). http://www.CBSNews.com.

Huffman, Mark. CARD ACT Could Impact Your Credit Score, http://www.ConsumerAffairs.com. (March 22, 2010).

Ivins, Molly. "Bad to Worse." (March 3, 2005). http://www.WorkingForChange.com.

Jackson, David. "Obama Looks to Avoid Fight Over New Consumer Agency." (September 16, 2010). http://www.USAToday.com.

Jakim, Boris and Laury Magnus, translators. *The Religious Poetry of Vladimir Solovyov*. San Rafael: CA, 2008.

Jesep, Paul Peter. *Crucifying Jesus and Secularizing America – the Republic of Faith without Wisdom*. Xlibris, 2008.

_____. "Stop Financial Vampirism," *Portsmouth Herald*, October 19, 2001.

_____. "Spiritual Leaders: Rise Up vs. Usury." *Portsmouth Herald*, June 22, 2003.

John Paul II. *Go in Peace*. Chicago: Loyola Press, 2003.

Jones, David W. *Reforming the Morality of Usury A Study of Differences that Separated the Protestant Reformers*. Dallas: University Press of America, 2004.

Kennedy, Bruce. "Could You Be a Victim of Credit Score Backlash?" (June 26, 2010). http://www.DailyFinance.com.

Kadlec, Dan. "Poor Credit Can Cost Your Kids their First Job." (October 20, 2010). http://www.MoneyWatch.bnet.com.

Kilpi, Jukka. *The Ethics of Bankruptcy*. London: Routledge, 1998.

Konczal, Mike. "Should You Trust Visa to Teach You About Credit Cards?" *Atlantic* (November 17, 2009). http://www.TheAtlantic.com.

Kraft, Stephanie. "Killer Loans – Student Loan Borrowers Drown in Debt as lenders make Billions." (October 14, 2010). http://www.ValleyAdvocate.com/article_print.cfm?aid=12585.

Kranish, Michael. "Push to Curb Credit-Card Rates Fades." (November 18, 2009). http://www.Boston.com.

Kroll, Andy. "Bank Bailout: The Greatest Swindle Ever Sold." (May 27, 2009). http://www.Salon.com.

Langel, Jesse. "Citibank (SD) NA Must Show Legal Support for Its Usurious Interest Rates." (June 16, 2010). http://www.TheLangelFirm.com.

Langer, Gary. "On Politics, Economy and the American Dream." (September 21, 2010). http://www.ABCNews.com.

LeMasters, Fr. Philip. *The Goodness of God's Creation – A Guide to Orthodox Ethics*. Salisbury, MA: Regina Orthodox Press, 2008.

Liberto, Jennifer and David Ellis. "Wall Street Reform: What's in the Bill." (June 25, 2010). http://www.CNNMoney.com.

Lieber, Ron and Tara Siegel Bernard. "From Card Fees to Mortgages, a New Day for Consumers." (June 25, 2010). http://www.NYTimes.com

Limbach, James. *Consumers Union Urges Rollback of Recent Credit Card Interest Rate Hikes.* (April 16, 2010). http://www.ConsumerAffairs.com.

Little, Lyneka. "Defining America's New Face of Poverty." (September 21, 2010). http://www.ABCNews.com

Lorber, Janie. "Amendments Target Credit Card Industry." Reprint from the *New York Times* Blog (May 12, 2010). http://www.whitehouse.senate.gov.

Lull, Timothy F. and William R. Russell, eds., *Martin Luther's Basic Theological Writings*. Minneapolis: Augsburg Fortress, 2005.

MacDonald, G. Jeffrey. "The Moral Burden of Bankruptcy," *Christian Science Monitor* (July 3, 2006). http://www.CSMonitor.com.

MacFarquhar, Neil. "Big Banks Draw Profits from Microloans to Poor." (April 13, 2010). http://www.NYTimes.com.

Maloney, Robert P. "The Teaching of the Fathers on Usury: An Historical Study on the Development of Christian Thinking," *Vigiliae Christianae* 27, No. 4 (December 1973): 241-265.

Mangu-Ward, Katherine. "Money Needed, Right Now." (June 25, 2010). http://www.wsj.com.

Mann, Ronald J. "Bankruptcy Reform and the Sweat Box of Credit Card Debt." *University of Illinois Law Review* 376 (2007).

_____. "Patterns of Credit Card Use Among Low and Moderate Income Households." http://www.Columbia.edu.

_____. "Saving Up for Bankruptcy." 98 *Georgetown Law Journal* 289 (2010).

*Marquette Nat. Bank v. First of Omaha Corp.*, 439 U.S. 299 (1978).

Marshall, Jr., Richard H. and Thomas E. Bird, eds. *Hryhorij Savyc Skovoroda – An Anthology of Critical Articles*. Edmonton: Canadian Institute of Ukrainian Studies Press, 1994.

Martelle, Scott. "Amid Lack of Jobs, Suicide Hot Line Calls Surge." (July 6, 2010). http://www.AOLNews.com.

Martin, Rachel. "President Obama Criticizes Mitch McConnell in Finance Reform Push," (April 17, 2010). http://www.ABCNews.com.

Martin, Renee. "In Minnesota Debtors' Prison is Not a Thing of the Past," http://www.GlobalComment.com, June 24, 2010.

Martin, Robert with Shelby Russ and Faye Robins. "Where's the Proof?" District Council 37 New York City Municipal Employees Legal Services," December 2009.

Martos, Joseph. *Door to the Sacred – A Historical Introduction to Sacraments In the Catholic Church.* New York: Doubleday & Company, Inc., 1981.

Mathews, Constantine. *Eastern Orthodoxy Compared.* Minneapolis: Light & Life Publishing Company, 2006.

Matlow, Daniel W. and Jamie B. Wasserman. "Hybrid Debt/Equity Transactions: Do They Intersect with the Usury Laws?" *Florida Bar Journal* 84, No. 4 (2010).

Mays, James L., General Editor. *The HarperCollins Bible Commentary.* San Francisco: HarperSanFrancisco, 2000.

McArdle, Megan. "FICO Frenzy." *The Atlantic* (August 17, 2010). http://www.TheAtlantic.com.

McGrane, Victoria. "Feinberg: Unfair to Ask Firms to Return Payouts." (July 23, 2010). http://www..wsj.com.

_____. "US Senate Nixes Plan to Let States Cap Interest Rates on National Banks." (May 19, 2010). http://www.nasdaq.com.

Men, Alexander. *Awake to Life! Sermons form the Paschal Cycle* Torrance, CA: Oakwood Publications, 1996.

_____. *About Christ and the Church*. Torrance: Oakwood Publications, 1996.

_____. *Christianity for the Twenty-First Century*. New York: Continuum, 1996.

_____. *Son of Man*. Torrance: Oakwood Publications, 1998.

Mencimer, Stephanie. "Christians Heart Payday Lenders," *Mother Jones* (March 5, 2008). http://www.MotherJones.com.

Metzger, Bruce M. and Michael D. Coogan. *The Oxford Companion to the Bible* New York: Oxford University Press, 1993.

Meyendorff, John. *St. Gregory Palamas and Orthodox Spirituality*. Crestwood: St. Vladimir's Seminary Press, 1993.

Miller, John W. *Meet the Prophets*. New York: Paulist Press, 1987.

Morgan, David S. "Warren: Middle Class Has Suffered for 30 Years." (September 21, 2010). http://www.CBSNews.com.

MSN Money Staff. "Your 5-Minute Guide to Credit Scores." (March 18, 2010). http://www.MoneyCentral.MSN.com.

Mueller, Karin Price. "Assessment Needed Before Canceling a Credit Card." (April 17, 2010). http://www.DelawareOnline.com.

Mui, Ylan Q. "The New Couple on Campus: Student Loan and Debit Card." (October 4, 2010). http://www.WashingtonPost.com.

Mulligan, John E. "Senate Kills Whitehouse Bill for Limits on Credit-Card Rates." *The Providence Journal* (May 21, 2010). http://www.ProJo.com.

Murray, Sara. "Employer Credit Checks on Job Seekers Draw Scrutiny." (October 21, 2010). http://www.WSJ.com.

National Association of Consumer Bankruptcy Attorneys. "Bankruptcy Reform's Impact: Where Are All the Deadbeats." (February 22, 2006).

*The New Oxford Annotated Bible.* Oxford: Oxford University Press, 2007.

New York City Bar Association. "Out of Service – A Call to Fix the Broken Process Service Industry," April 2010.

New York State Attorney General's Office. "No Rhyme or Reason: The 'Heads I Win, Tails You Lose' Bank Bonus Culture," Report. July 30, 2009.

Nikodimos of the Holy Mountain and Makarios of Corinth. *The Philokalia Vol. Two.* London: Faber and Faber, 1984.

Novack, Janet. "Credit Card Debt Blamed for Surge in Elder Bankruptcy." (October 12, 2010). http://www.Forbes.com.

O'Collins, Gerald and Edward G. Farrugia. *A Concise Dictionary of Theology*. New York: Paulist Press, 2000.

O'Donovan, Oliver and Joan Lockwood O'Donovan. *Bonds of Imperfection: Christian Politics, Past and Present.* Grand Rapids: Wm. B. Eerdmans Publishing Company, 2003.

Orlian, Rabbi Meir. "The Usury Suspects." (printed September 22, 2010, copyright 2010). http://www.Communitym.com.

*Orthodox Study Bible* (New King James Version). Edited and Annotated by His Beatitude Metropolitan MAXIMOS, Michel Najim, and Joseph Allen. Nashville: Thomas Nelson, 2008.

"Pay Czar: 17 Bailed-Out Banks Overpaid Execs." (July 23, 2010). http://www.CBSNews.com.

Papanikolaou, Aristole and Elizabeth H. Prodromou, eds. *Think through Faith – New perspectives from Orthodox Christian Scholars*. Crestwood: St. Vladimir's Seminary Press, 2008.

Parramore, Lynn. "Exclusive Interview: Elizabeth Warren Says Big Banks Must Stop Blocking Reform." (July 12, 2010). http://www.HuffingtonPost.com.

Paul, Peralte C. "Katrina Victims Unlikely to Get Break on New Bankruptcy Law," (September 22, 2005). http://www.AJC.com.

Pennington, M. Basil. *The Eucharist – Wine of Faith Bread of Life* (Liguori, MO: Liguori/Triumph, 2000.

Perkins, Francesca J. "South Dakota National Bank Denied Interest Rate in Excess of New York Usury Laws."(September 20, 2010). http://www.Lexology.com.

Phillips, Rich. "Woman Sues Debt Collector Over Husband's Death." (December 10, 2009). http://www.CNN.com.

Prater, Connie. "Poll: Credit Card Debt the New Taboo Topic." (July 1, 2008). http://www.CreditCards.com.

Price, Vedder, Laura Sack, and Roy P. Salins. "Employers Relying on Background Checks Face Increased Scrutiny." (August 6, 2010). http://www.Lexology.com.

Puzzanghera, Jim. "House, Senate Lawmakers Reach a Deal on Financial Reform." (June 25, 2010). http://www.LATimes.com.

Rappaport, Liz, Aaron Lucchetti and Stephen Grocer, "Wall Street Pay: A Record $144 Billion." (October 11, 2010). http://www.WSJ.com.

Reese, J. "Pope Benedict on Economic Justice." *Washington Post* (July 7, 2009). http://www.WashingtonPost.com.

Rodewald, Adam. "Student Loan Debt Now Exceeds Credit Cards." (October 21, 2010). http://www.TheNorthwestern.com.

Romanides, John. *An Outline of Orthodox Patristic Dogmatics*. Rollinsford, New Hampshire: Orthodox Research Institute, 2004.

Roshau, Christie. "Credit Card Reform Law's Impact on Campus: 'What Law'?" (May 11, 2010). http://www.CreditCards.com.

Rudolf, John Collins. "Pay Garnishments Rise as Debtors Fall Behind." *New York Times* (April 1, 2010). http://www.NYTimes.com.

Ruiz, Michelle. "Vile Voice Mails Cost Agency." (June 2, 2010). http://www.AOLNews.com.

"Salvation Army Kettles Now Take Plastic." (November 25, 2009). http://www.MSNBC.com.

Sandel, Michael J. *Justice – What's the Right Thing to Do?* New York: Farrar, Straus and Giroux, 2009.

Schipflinger, Thomas. *Sophia-Maria – A Holistic Vision of Creation*. York Beach, Maine: Samuel Weiser, Inc., 1998.

Schoen, John W. "Bad Credit Sidelines some Jobless Workers." (February 23, 2010). http://www.MSNBC.com.

Scott, Matthew. "Is Debt a New Form of Slavery?" (October 21, 2010). http://www.DailyFinance.com.

Sen, Amartya. *On Ethics & Economics*. Malden, MA: Blackwell Publishing, 1988.

_____. *The Idea of Justice*. Cambridge: Harvard University Press, 2009.

Serres, Chris. "Death Won't Stop These Debt Collectors."
(September 22, 2010). http://www/StarTribune.com

_____. "In Jail for Being in Debt." StarTribune.com
(June 9, 2010). http://www.StarTribune.com.

"Is Senate Proposal Death Knell for 30% Credit-Card Rates."
(May 19, 2010). http://www.ConsumerReports.org.

Sheen, Fulton J. *Your Life is Worth Living*. Schnecksville, PA:
St. Andrew's Press, 2001.

Shenon, Philip. "America's Worst Credit Card." (October 19,
2010). http://www.TheDailyBeast.com.

Sider, Ronald J. *The Scandal of the Evangelical Conscience*. Grand
Rapids: Baker Books, 2005.

_____ and Diane Knippers, eds. *Toward An Evangelical Public
Policy*. Grand Rapids: BakerBooks, 2005.

Silver-Greenberg, Jessica. "The New Credit-Card Tricks." (July
31, 2010). http://www.online.wsj.com.

Smith, Charles Hugh. "Recession Over? Household Balance
Sheets Tell a Different Story." (September 22, 2010).
http://www.DailyFinance.com.

Smith, Eva Norlyk. "Financial Reform Aims to Demystify
Credit Scores." (August 17, 2010).
http://www.CreditCardGuide.com.

_____. "Why Are the Three Credit Bureaus Scores Different?" (September 28, 2009). http://www.CreditCardguide.com.

Solovey, Meletius. *A Commentary on the Byzantine Liturgy*. Warren, MI: Basilian Fathers Publications, 1989.

Solovyov, Vladimir. *Divine Humanity*. Hudson, NY: Lindisfarne Press, 1995.

Springen, Karen. "Going for Broke." (August 31, 2006). http://www.MSNBC.com.

Stein, Robin. "The Ascendancy of the Credit Card Industry." *Frontline* (November 23, 2004). http://www.PBS.org.

Stephey, M.J. "A Brief History of: Credit Cards." *Time* (April 23, 2009). http://www.Time.com.

Stern, Linda. "A New Shakedown?" *Newsweek* (July 21, 2008). http://www.Newsweek.com.

Stolberg, Sheryl Gay. "Obama Vows to Move on Regulation." *New York Times* (April 17, 2010). http://www.NYTimes.com.

Story, Louise and Gretchen Morgenson, "For Goldman, a Bet's Stakes Keep Growing." *New York Times* (April 17, 2010). http://www.NYTimes.com.

Stout, David. "Senate Passes Bill to Restrict Credit-Card Practices." *New York Times* (May 20, 2009). http://www.NYTimes.com.

Streitfeld, David. "Biggest Defaulters on Mortgages Are the Rice." (July 8, 2010). http://www.NYTimes.com.

Strong, James. *The Strong's Exhaustive Concordance of the Bible.* Nashville: Thomas Nelson Publishers, 1996.

"Student-Loan Debt Surpasses Credit Cards," *Wall Street Journal* (blogs.wsj.com), August 9, 2010.

Sturgeon, Julie. "Bad Credit Hurts in Many Ways." (June 16, 2008). http://www.Bankrate.com.

Sullivan, Bob. "The Red Tape Chronicles – Are Clinic Visits on Credit Reports?" (May 9, 2006). http://www..MSNBC.com.

_____. "The Red Tape Chronicles – The New Consumer Agency: What's in it for You." (July 21, 2010). http://www.MSNBC.com.

_____. "The Red Tape Chronicles – For Teacher, A Tough Lesson In Debt Settlement." (May 25, 2010). http://www.MSNBC.com.

_____. "The Red Tape Chronicles – What's in Your Wallet? A Big Loophole." (September 7, 2010). http://www.MSNBC.com.

Sullivan, Teresa A., Elizabeth Warren, and Jay Lawrence Westbrook. *The Fragile Middle Class – Americans in Debt.* New Haven: Yale University Press, 2000.

Szpek, Heidi M. *Voices from the University: The Legacy of the Hebrew Bible.* Bloomington IL: iUniverse, 2002.

Telvick, Mariena. "Charge It." *Frontline*. http://www.PBS.org (accessed July 2009).

―――――. "Examining the Issue of Credit Cards and Personal Responsibility." *Frontline*. http://www.PBS.org (accessed March 17, 2007).

Thompson, Carolyn and David B. Caruso. "Buffalo's Debt Collectors Accused of Bullying." *Associated Press* (January 5, 2010).

Tolstoy, Leo. *A Confession and Other Religious Writings*. London: Penguin Books, 1987.

―――――. *The Kingdom of God is Within You*. Mineola, New York: Dover Publications, 2006.

Todorova, Aleksandra. "Credit Card Companies Are…" http://www.SmartMoney.com (accessed August 10, 2005).

*The Traditional Latin Roman Catholic Mass*. New York: C.T.M. Publications, 1977.

"UAW and Religious Leaders Plan to Pull Millions of Dollars From JPMorgan Chase," (September 24, 2010). http://www.WXYZ.com.

Underhill, Evelyn. *Abba – Meditations Based on the Lord's Prayer*. New York: Vintage Books, 2003.

U.S. Catholic Bishops. *Pastoral Letter on Catholic Social Teaching and the U.S. Economy*. Office for Social Justice, 1986.

Valliere, Paul. *Bukharev, Soloviev, Bulgakov*. Grand Rapids: William B. Eerdmans Publishing Company, 2000.

Van Biema, David and Jeff Chu. "Does God Want You to Be Rich." *Time* (September 10, 2006). http://www.Time.com

Vance, Karen. "Archdiocese Passes Online Plate." (December 24, 2007). http://www.News.Enquirer.com.

Vekshin, Alison. "Credit-Card Fees Hurt American Consumers, Senators Tell Issuers." (March 7, 2007). http://www.Bloomberg.com.

"Vile Voice Mails Cost Agency $1.5 Million." (June 2, 2010). http://www.AOLNews.com.

Visser, Wayne A.M. and Alastair McIntosh. "A Short Review of the Historical Critique of Usury." *Accounting, Business & Financial History* 8, no.2 (1998).

Von Hoffman, Nicholas. "Credit Card Tricks." *The Nation* (March 16, 2007).

Vysheslavtsev, B.P. *The Eternal in Russian Philosophy*. Grand Rapids: W. B. Eerdmans Publishing Co., 2002.

"Wall Street Faces N.Y. Probe on Ratings Data." (May 13, 2010). http://www. Money.CNN.com.

Wallace, Charles. "Consumers Face Huge Losses with Debt Settlement Firms." (August 31, 2010). http://www.DailyFinance.com.

———————. "Losses Mount as Debt Settlement Firms Face New Rules." (September 13, 2010). http://www.DailyFinance.com.

Walter, Jennifer. "Another Shoe to Drop – Bad Credit-Card Debt Could Be Next Shot to Economy, Researcher Says." (September 30, 2008).

Warren, Elizabeth. "Secret History of the Credit Card." *Frontline*. http://www.WMHT.com (accessed March 17, 2007).

Watkins, Thomas. "Indebted Troops Spending Time Out of Harm's Way." *Denver Post* (October 19, 2006). http://www.DenverPost.com.

Watson, Bruce. "The 10 Biggest Corporate Campaign Contributors in U.S. Politics." (October 13, 2010). http://www.DailyFinance.com.

———————. "Disturbing Statistics on the Decline of America's Middle Class." (October 17, 2010). http://www.DailyFinance.com.

Weisbaum, Herb. "Job Candidates Undergoing Credit Scrutiny." (August 4, 2010). http://www.MSNBC.com.

———————. "Warren's Top Goal: Keeping Credit Simple." (September 22, 2010). http://www.MSNBC.com.

Weisenthal, Joe. "A Case for Capping Credit Card Rates." (April 23, 2009). http://www.BusinessInsider.com.

Weston, Liz Pulliam. "8 Secret Scores that Lenders Keep." (March 17, 2009). http://www.MoneyCentral.msn.com.

_____. "Zombie Debt is hard to Kill." http://Articles.MoneyCentral.MSNBC.com. (accessed August 2, 2006).

"What You Buy Affects Your Credit." http://www.WalletPop.com (accessed August 2009).

White, Martha C. "America's New Debtor Prison: Jail Time being Given to those Who Owe." http://www.WalletPop.com (July 15, 2010).

_____. "Good Credit Score Secrets." (July 7, 2010). http://www.WalletPop.com.

"Whitehouse Statement on Senate Vote on Marquette Amendment," (May 19, 2010). http://whitehouse.senate.gov.

Williams, Julie (Interview with). "Secret History of the Credit Card." Frontline. http://www.WMHT.com (accessed March 17, 2007).

Wills, Gary. *What Jesus Meant*. New York: Penguin Books, 2007.

_____. *What the Gospels Meant*. New York: Penguin Group, 2008.

Woolsey, Ben and Matt Schutz. "Credit Card Statistics, Industry Facts, Debt Statistics." http://www.CreditCards.com (accessed May 2009).

"Worst: First Premier Bank Mastercard." http://www.ConsumerReports.org. (November 2010).

Wriston, Walter (Interview with). "Secret History of the Credit Card." Frontline. http://www.WMHT.com (accessed March 17, 2007).

Yingling, Edward (Interview with). "Secret History of the Credit Card." Frontline. (March 17, 2007). http://www.WMHT.com.

York, Kate. "Average FICO Score Drops Below 600." (July 25, 2010). http://www.NewsAndSentinel.com.

Zehr, Howard. *The Little Book of Restorative Justice*. Intercourse, PA: Good Books, 2002.

Zuckerman, Gregory. "Heard on the Street: Debt Collectors Reap Rewards As Consumers Rack Up Bills." (November 2, 2004). http://www.WSJ.com.

# Index

| | |
|---|---|
| Americans for Fairness in Lending | 43 |
| Aristotle | 9, 62, 63, 74 |
| Atlanta Legal Aid | 44 |
| Barclay, William | 27, 91 |
| Basil of Caesarea | 76 |
| Benedict XVI | 41, 77 |
| Beneficial | 44 |
| Better Business Bureau | 50, 123 |
| Blumenthal, Richard | 47 |
| Bond, Julian | 23 |
| Buffalo | 50 |
| Capital One | 43 |
| Capitalism | 7, 21, 29, 55 |
| Catholic Archdiocese of Cincinnati | 26 |
| Ciaffa, Judge Michael | 51, 52 |
| Citibank | 12, 52 |
| Citigroup | 39 |
| Civil Rights | 33, 34, 93 |
| Cohen & Slamowitz | 52 |
| Collection Agencies | 7, 9, 18, 49, 50, 51, 57, 64, 83, 88, 90, 92 |
| Commoditization | 25, 60 |
| Connecticut Attorney General | 47 |
| Consumer Bankruptcy Attorneys | 29, 30 |
| Consumer Financial Protection Agency | 47 |
| Contract with America | 25, 26 |
| Copeland, Gloria | 22 |
| Corporate Responsibility | 55, 56 |
| Credit Bureaus | 7, 9, 18, 32, 33, 36, 49, 88, 90, 92 |

| | |
|---|---|
| Credit Card Accountability, Responsibility and Disclosure Act | 45 |
| Credit Scores | 32, 33, 36, 37, 38, 40, 62, 88 |
| Cuomo, Andrew | 38, 39 |
| Darwinian Capitalism | 7, 55 |
| Debtor's Prison | 54 |
| Debt Stress Syndrome | 41, 66 |
| Discover | 42 |
| Eastern Baptist Theological Seminary | 24, 80 |
| Eltman, Eltman & Cooper | 51 |
| Eucharist | 17, 18, 20, 28, 58, 59, 60, 61, 62, 64, 68, 72, 74, 80, 83, 86 |
| Fair Debt Collection Practices Act | 48 |
| Fair Isaac Credit Organization (FICO) | 7, 36, 37, 38, 39, 56 |
| Federal Reserve | 46, 47, 87 |
| Federal Trade Commission | 26, 50, 89 |
| Forrester, Duncan B. | 63 |
| Goldman Sachs | 32, 39 |
| Gregory of Nazianzus | 76 |
| Gregory of Nyssa | 76 |
| Gulf Coast | 90 |
| John Chrysostom | 59, 73 |
| John Paul II | 59 |
| J.P. Morgan Chase | 32, 39 |
| Jubilation, Jubilee | 17, 69, 73, 75, 90 |
| Katrina | 31, 90 |
| King, Jr., Martin Luther | 62 |
| Long, Eddie | 23 |
| Lynch, Merrill | 39 |
| Mann, Ronald J. | 30, 78 |

| | |
|---|---|
| MBNA | 43 |
| McConnell, Mitch | 31 |
| Minnesota | 54 |
| Morgan Stanley | 32, 39 |
| Mystical Supper | 19, 28, 58, 60, 68, 83, 92 |
| NAACP | 23 |
| National Association of Consumer Bankruptcy Attorneys | 29 |
| National Consumer Law Center | 40 |
| New York Attorney General | 38, 39, 51 |
| New York City Bar Association | 53 |
| New York City Municipal Employees Legal Services | 52, 89 |
| Nikodimos and Makarios | 63, 80 |
| Obama, Barack | 11, 31, 32 |
| Personal Responsibility | 31, 55, 56, 57, 92 |
| Peters, Rebecca Todd | 25 |
| Peterson, Christopher | 24 |
| Philokalia | 63 |
| Prosperity Gospel | 22, 23, 24, 26, 61, 70 |
| Sacralization | 21, 60 |
| Salvation Army | 26 |
| Securities and Exchange Commission | 39 |
| Sen, Amartya | 62, 63 |
| Sheptytsky, Andrey | 86 |
| Sider Center on Ministry and Public Policy | 24, 80 |
| Society of Human Resource Management | 34 |
| Southern Baptist Convention | 24 |
| Straniere, Judge Philip | 52 |
| Student Loans | 7, 59 |
| Suicide Awareness Voices of Education | 42 |
| Tikhon of Zadonsk | 71 |

| | |
|---|---|
| Troubled Asset Relief Program (TARP) | 39 |
| Unjust Gain | 8, 13, 17, 28, 57, 59, 70, 75, 92 |
| U.S. Catholic Conference of Bishops | 19 |
| U.S. Public Interest Research Group | 15 |
| Usury | 12, 25, 52, 76, 87 |
| Vatican Council II | 19 |
| Vysheslavtsev, Boris | 60, 61 |
| Warren, Elizabeth | 10, 11, 13, 30, 77 |

# Scriptural References

| | |
|---|---|
| Amos | 2:6-7; 5:6-7; 5:14; 5:18-20 |
| 1 Chronic | 10:26; 29:11 |
| 1 Corinthians | 10:26; 11:27 |
| Deuteronomy | 6:25; 10:14; 15:1-11; 15:15; 24:12-13, 17 |
| Exodus | 19:5; 22:25 |
| Genesis | 1:1 |
| Haggai | 2:8 |
| Isaiah | 5:17; 58:6 |
| Jeremiah | 15:10 |
| Job | 41:11 |
| John | 2:13-16; 12:36 |
| 2 Kings | 4:1-7 |
| Leviticus | 19:18; 25:1-55; 25:23; 25:42-43 |
| Luke | 4:18-21; 17:20-21; 19:45-48; 20:1-8; 22:14-23 |
| Mark | 11:15-19; 11:27-33; 14:22-26; 14:35-36 |
| Matthew | 4:8-9; 5:13-14; 5:43-46; 7:12; 18:21; 21:12-17; 21:23-2; 26:26-29 |
| Micah | 3:5-7 |
| Psalm | 24:1; 133:1 |
| Proverbs | 23:4; 28:20 |
| 1 Thessalonians | 5:5 |

# Links and Resources

### Americans for Fairness in Lending
http://www.affil.org
AFFIL is a 200 plus coalition of local, state, and national groups that seeks reform in banking and financial services.

### BC Alliance
http://www.bcsalliance.com/index.html
The Alliance answers questions about your rights and filing complaints against credit card companies, among other things.

### Better Business Bureau
http://www.bbb.org/us/
It seeks to further ethical commercial transactions between buyers and sellers. It is also a place where consumers can file complaints against businesses.

### Center for Responsible Lending
http://www.responsiblelending.org/
Starting in 2002, the Center for Responsible Lending (CRL) has, according to its website, "protected homeownership and family wealth by working to eliminate abusive financial practices."

### Consumer Federation of America
http://www.consumerfed.org/
Approximately 280 nonprofits make up its membership. It tries to empower those most likely to be oppressed and disseminates information to policymakers.

### Consumer Rights Lawyers
http://naca.networkats.com/members_online/members/directorya.asp?token=
If you need a consumer rights attorney to sue a creditor then try this link.

**Credit.com**
http://www.Credit.com
Credit.com provides credit information to consumers.

**CreditCards.com**
http://www.CreditCards.com
CreditCards.com monitors the credit card market providing valuable data and statistics.

**Debt Prison**
http://www.DebtPrison.net
Debt Prison helps consumers liberate themselves from consumer credit exploitation.

**Federal Trade Commission**
http://www.ftc.gov/bcp/menus/consumer/credit/loans.shtm
Federal agency that provides information on credit cards and consumer rights.

**Low Cards**
http://www.LowCards.com
According to its website Low Cards is "the leading consumer resource for credit card information."

**Open Secrets**
http://www.OpenSecrets.org
Good government group that tracks the donations received by Congressional lawmakers. This includes donations made by the financial services industry seeking to influence legislation.

## Student Loan Debt and Exploitation
http://www.StudentLoanJustice.org
http://www.ForgiveStudentLoanDebt.com
http://www. BankruptYourStudentLoans.com
Student loan debt is another injustice that Christian leaders should address. Students are encouraged to "invest in their future" by taking out massive amounts of loans despite the hard reality that they will not earn a suitable income to pay off the debt with any ease, if at all. Like those with credit cards, graduates will become a cash cow, a long-term revenue source for banks.

## 10 Percent Is Enough
http://www.10PercentIsEnough.org
http://www.Industrialareasfoundation.org
10 Percent Is Enough was started by the Metro Industrial Areas Foundation, a coalition of 17 "broad-based citizen organizations." Its achievements have included a living wage law in Baltimore county, construction of over 5,000 Nehemiah homes in several cities, and passage of universal healthcare in the Commonwealth of Massachusetts.

## US Public Interest Research Groups (PIRGs)
http://www.USPIRG.org
Consumer advocate/good government group with chapters throughout the country confronts special interest groups that attempt to influence legislation that harms Americans.

# About the Author

Paul Peter Jesep is an ordained priest and consecrated bishop in the Orthodox Church. Bishop Jesep, by appointment of His Beatitude Metropolitan Myfodii of Kyiv and All Rus-Ukraine, is Director of Public Affairs for the Ukrainian Autocephalous Orthodox Church (UAOC) Kyiv-Patriarchate in the United States. The UAOC is Ukraine's third largest Orthodox Church.

Bishop Jesep earned a B.A. in political science from Union College in New York, a J.D. from Western New England College School of Law in Massachusetts, a Master of Professional Management from the Graduate School of Political Management now based at The George Washington University, and a Master of Arts from Bangor Theological Seminary in Maine.

He is a practicing attorney in New York State and author of *Crucifying Jesus and Secularizing America - the Republic of Faith without Wisdom*. The views expressed by Bishop Jesep in his written works and public comments are personal and do not necessarily reflect the official position of the UAOC. Contact him at VladykaPaulPeter@aol.com.

Made in the USA
Lexington, KY
25 April 2011